EXTREME RAFTING

Maurizio Bernasconi
Marco Tenucci

◆

EXTREME RAFTING

HISTORY, TECHNIQUES, RUNS

UNIVERSE PUBLISHING

Contents

Rafting

The Mississippi River is the stage for the adventures of Huckleberry Finn, who escapes from the risks of civilization and the rigors of a conventional education to go down the river on a raft – saying that it is certainly a great life on a raft, spending a whole day going down the river doing nothing.

Most probably the raft appealed to Twain because of its easy maneuverability and transport. It is the ideal means to go down rivers in an adventurous and exciting way, running rapids, being close to nature, the fluvial scenery, learning about the riverside inhabitants and settlements.

A raft is a flat floating structure, usually made of pieces of wood tied together, which is used as a boat. It is certainly the origin of today's inflatable river raft, known as an inflatable canoe or raft, and is nothing more than a water craft able to float because it has been filled with air.

THE RAFT
It is an inflatable craft without rigid parts which looks more or less like a canoe. The synthetic material used in its manufacture makes it unsinkable and very light. It is easy to maneuver even by people who want to attempt a river run and who don't know much about the complex methods of paddling a canoe or kayak. The tourist use of river inflatables has increased enormously in the last twenty years, exactly for this reason: as non-experts they can run fairly "easy" torrents without too many risks.

HOBBY OR EXTREME ACTIVITY
Runs down a river that are not too difficult are within everyone's capabilities, even children's. The more demanding runs, instead, are for athletes who are able to tackle the dangers of the fastest rivers; at that point rafting is considered an extreme sport where you are challenging yourself to the limit.

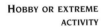

RUNS IN CANOES OR INFLATABLE RAFTS
They are two completely different sports and are not comparable. A canoe can maneuver in rapids while an inflatable is slower, more cumbersome, and less acrobatic. However, both canoes and rafts frequently run the same rivers, exploiting their particular characteristics. The inflatable, because of its size and stability, is used to transport equipment and baggage, while canoes and kayaks, because of their maneuverability, are used for rescue or recovery.

Origins of the raft

It could be said that the first man to cling on to a floating trunk and try to steer it started river navigation. From the earliest times, the need to cross and go up and down rivers has pushed man to hollow out trunks to make rudimentary canoes, or to tie them together to make rafts for transportation. Even in ancient times, there were marked differences between boats used on rivers and those used for marine navigation.

THE ANCIENT EGYPTIANS
From paintings found in excavated tombs, as can be seen above in *The Fisherman with a Harpoon*, the Egyptians constructed rafts by tying reeds together, but these were only suitable for river navigation. The sailing boats seen in other paintings are suitable for use at sea. In Egypt the concept of charity toward those without a boat is a very old one. The book of *The Teachings of Amenemope* warns: "Never leave behind a man in the passage of a river when you have space on the ferry boat. Do not build a boat and try to get the toll: Ask for the toll from those that have it and refuse it from those that cannot afford it."

TRUNK FLOATING
This is a practice that goes back to ancient times in many countries in the world. The current is used to transport the trunks, which are either left at the mercy of the river, or are cut and tied together to form enormous rafts. When this happens the lumbermen get on board and navigate using long bamboo poles.

THE FERRYMAN
He is a symbolic and literary figure and in many parts of the world, from Nepal to Venice, still has a very important role to play.

BOATS MADE FROM SKIN

Goat and other animal skins were used by many primitive peoples and are still used today in some regions of Asia. The picture shows a traditional boat made from yak skin used to cross the Lhasa He River in Tibet.

RAFTS MADE FROM INFLATED SKINS

These can be considered the precedent of today's rafts. It seems that even Alexander the Great crossed the Indo rapids using inflatable boats made from cow and horse hides sewed, inflated, and then waterproofed with animal fat. The first example of such a raft dates from 880 B.C. and is exhibited at the British Museum in London. In Pakistan, rafts made from inflated goat stomachs are still used to cross the Shigar River.

CANOES

Their shape has remained similar since ancient times. The canoe exhibited at the Ethnographic Museum in Mexico City is not so different from others found around the world.

INNER TUBES

Inner tubes can be used in low grade (levels I and II) rivers and streams. Care should be used and knowledge of the watercourse is strongly recommended. Tubers should ride in pairs for safety.

The first inflatable river boats

Around the middle of the 19th century a famous British sailing company designed an inflatable rubber boat which was tested among the ice of the North Pole. In the same period, an American named Peter Halket designed a boat made of a cotton air chamber coated with rubber and covered with canvas. In the following decades, both in the United States and in Europe, these crafts were used for military purposes. In 1918, canvas-covered craft were used for the German invasion of Libya; then in 1922, the Floossboot of Berlin produced inflatable rafts that were used for transporting tanks on rivers.

The builders of ocean liners opted for inflatable craft for safety reasons during the second half of the fifties, after the sinking of the *Andrea Doria* had demonstrated how unsuitable normal lifeboats were for rescue.

THE GEORGIE WHITE COMPANY

This was the first company to organize runs in 1951 down the Colorado. Basically, it was an initiative for a few adventurous people who wanted to spend a couple of weeks going down the Colorado, as the pioneers did. Very soon these runs began to attract an ever-increasing number of tourists. They became so popular that in 1972, the National Park Service capped the maximum number of people at 17,000 per year, to try to limit the environmental damage to this river.

RAFTING ORGANIZATIONS

As a result of the enormous success of river runs, soon other rivers were explored. Smaller boats were built that could be used with oars or paddles. Without the rigid structure of the larger boat, rafts were more able to absorb the impact of the waves. With these improved rafts it became possible to go down smaller rivers, even steeper and wilder than the Colorado. Other organizations followed the example of Georgie White and rafting changed from its original pioneering spirit, into an organized tourist and sport activity. In the United States in 1985, there were more than 400,000 "rafters" and more than 150 outfitters. Today it has become so widespread that it's impossible to give any precise figures. On every watercourse where it's possible to descend there are rafting schools, and it's not unusual to see even Bill Clinton, with his daughter and some bodyguards, running a rapid in an inflatable.

In 1857, Lt. Ives, on his return from the Colorado, commented on the failure of the government expedition he had led: "This was the first and last expedition to go down the Grand Canyon, as nature has decided that it should remain virgin for ever." It was not until 1869 that the military mission led by John Wesley Powell was successfully able to go down these wild rapids. Only a few people were able to repeat this feat, until 1950, when the first motor rafts started to be used.

Inflatable river boats in Russia

There are still places where rafting has not yet become a tourist phenomenon organized by specialized companies. In the Urals and the Caucasus Hills, Dagestan, Siberia, and Georgia, the pioneering spirit still exists. In these regions there is still a tradition of running rivers on inflatable craft made by the runners. Often, there are whole families that run the rivers on cheap catamarans and travel through valleys covered with birch trees. For some time now in these regions, it has become customary for the adventuresome to descend the more impetuous rivers aboard inflatable dinghies that are built by the river navigators themselves.

TRANSPORT
The Russians organize trips either by truck or train for hundreds of miles to the put-in. These rivers are beautiful places with crystal clear waters and unspoilt countryside.

RUSSIAN CHAMPIONS
The rafts used in these places, however rudimentary, are so well constructed that they are able to tackle even the most difficult runs. The real enthusiasts become very experienced and in European competitions are frequently in the top positions though competing with inferior equipment.

THE CATARAFT
The adventure begins with the construction of the raft: a resistant waterproof canvas, a suitable glue, and a valve system are needed. To make a classic raft can be complicated, while a cataraft made up of two tubes and four cones is much easier. The tubes can be joined by tubes of aluminium, which are light and easily obtained, or birch branches, which can be cut on the spot when assembling the raft.

From the USA to Europe

Statistics in the recent National Survey on Recreation and the Environment show that 13.2 million people do traditional canoeing, 1.4 million people use a river or sea kayak, and 15.2 million people do rafting. To go down the Colorado River in the Grand Canyon National Park there is a seven-year waiting list at the River Permit Office. To go down the Middle Fork on the Salmon River there is a draw to decide which of the 6,000 groups, of not more than 24 people each, will have the privilege of running the river on one of the 372 available dates. In 1968, about 5,000 people had run the Youghiogheny River, but today there are more than 120,000; there were 2,000 on the New River and today the number is not less than 100,000. Originally, those rivers had not been run. In the meantime, rafting has become a widespread sport, especially in Europe. Since 1982, French outfitters started to propose river trips on rivers in the Alps and the Massif Centrale in central Europe, and since 1987, the French Canoe and Kayak Federation has included rafting among its list of recognized river sports.

FLORENCE EXPEDITION
A small group of Florentine explorers, founded by Jacopo Mazzei in 1973, was the first to run the Blue Nile by raft down its 1054 miles (1,700 km) through Sudan and Ethiopia. Following this, members of the Florence Expedition also ran the Zaire around the Livingstone Falls, the Colorado, and the Zambezi. In 1984, they were the first to run the Alas River in Sumatra.

PROTECTED RESOURCES
The rivers that offer the best characteristics for descent (for example, those with a substantial amount of water most of the year) have been attracting ever-growing numbers of rafters. Naturally, this has influenced the tourist business so that rivers have come to be considered resources that have to be protected.

RIVER TRIPS
Rivers are severe natural environments that should be approached with a certain physical and mental preparation. Those professional outfitters that have been organizing river trips have discovered that they have become intermediaries between the public and the river.

Some European runs

DURANCE

In France, for some years, numerous outfitters have proposed runs on different rivers by raft, canoe, and hydrospeed. One of the best known, for the number of people who run it, is the Durance River because of the big volume of water and lack of dangerous parts. Here beginners, children, elderly people, and slightly handicapped people can run this river.

DORA BALTEA

This river is known as the Colorado of Europe because of the speed of the current and the strength of its rapids. The glaciers of Mont Blanc offer the rafter unique natural scenery and the run can take a river runner's breath away. The put-in is at the confluence of the Dora di Thuile at Sarre, and the run continues through an uninterrupted series of rapids, which, at the start, are very fast. The best period to run them is from May to September.

THE RHINE RIVER

This Alpine river brings to mind those in North America because of its magnificence, its impressiveness, and the geological formations of its gorges. Adding to the beauty of a run on the Rhine there are also the great distances involved in reaching a tarmacked road. One curiosity of this run is the possibility of recovering the inflatable by train.

SJÖA, NORWAY

This river runs through the unspoilt Heidal Valley where the green pastures are dotted only by farms, the traditional buildings of the farmers, and herds of wild reindeer. This river, considered to be the best in Scandinavia for rafting, flows through rapids that gradually become more demanding.

INN

Many rivers in Austria are fed by the abundant summer rainfall and the glaciers found everywhere, making this area one of the most frequented for wildwater. The Inn and its tributaries offer many miles of fast rapids and interesting runs. Austria is the ideal destination for those who want to run a high number of different runs.

Rafting in the USA

Alabama
- ALABAMA SMALL BOATS, INC
(Helena)
Tel. 205-424-3634
- SOUTHERN TRAILS, INC
(Montgomery)
Tel. 205-272-0952

Alaska
- ALASKA TRAVEL ADVENTURE
(Juneau)
Tel. 907-789-0052

Arkansas
- ARKATENTS USA/JUST US FLOATERS
(Mena)
Tel. 501-394-7893
- DODD'S CANOE RENTAL
(Yellville)
Tel. 501-449-6619
- MANY ISLANDS CAMP, INC
(Mammoth Spring)
Tel. 501-856-3451

Arizona
- CANYONS & COAST LINES KAYAK SCHOOL
(Phoenix)
Tel. 602-258-6318 - fax 602-254-8180

California
- AQUA ADVENTURE
(San Diego)
Tel. 619-272-0800 - fax 619-272-0800
- CALIFORNIA RIVERS PADDLESPORTS
(Windsor)
Tel. 707-838-8919
- KAYAK CONNECTION
(Santa Cruz)
Tel. 408-479-1121/408-724-5692

Colorado
- MOUNTAIN WATERS RAFTING
(Durango)
Tel. 970-259-4191/800-748-2507
- WILDERNESS AWARE RAFTING, INC
(Buena Vista)
Tel. 800-462-7238 - fax 719-395-6716

Connecticut
- CLARKE OUTDOOR, INC
(West Cornwall)
Tel. 860-672-6365

Delaware
- WILDERNESS CANOE TRIPS, INC
(Wilmington)
Tel. 302-654-2227

Georgia
- WHITE WATER LEARNING CENTER OF GA., INC
(Atlanta)
Tel. 404-231-0042 - fax 404-231-1199

Iowa
- OSTERDOCK OUTFITTERS
(Colesburg)
Tel. 319-252-2257

Illinois
- AMERICAN PIONEER CANOE, INC
(Roscoe)
Tel. 815-624-6285 - fax 815-624-8641

Indiana
- CANOE COUNTRY
(Daleville)
Tel. 317-378-7358/888-378-7358
- CAVE COUNTRY CANOES, INC
(Marengo)
Tel. 812-365-2058

Kansas
- YAKITI YAKS
(Augusta)
Tel. 316-775-5771

Kentucky
- PHILLIP GALLS
(Lexington)
Tel. 606-266-0469 - fax 606-269-5190
- SOUTH CENTRAL CANOE, INC
(Bowling Green)
Tel. 502-783-0233

Louisiana
- BIG CREEK OUTFITTERS & EXPEDITIONS, INC
(Pollock)
Tel. 318-765-3060

Massachussetts
- CHARLES RIVER CANOE & KAYAK
(Newton)
Tel. 617-965-5110 - fax 617-965-7696
- NASHOBA PADDLER
(West Groton)
Tel. 508-448-8699

Maryland
- POKOMOKE RIVER
(Snow Hill)
Tel. 410-632-3971

Maine
- PENOBSCOT RIVER OUTFITTERS
(Medway)
Tel. 207-746-9349

Michigan
- CHIPPEWA RIVER OUTFITTERS
(Mount Pleasant)
Tel. 517-772-5474
- MICHIGAN PADDLESPORTS & HOBBY
(Pinckney)
Tel. 313-426-1651

Minnesota
- SEAGULL OUTFITTERS
(Grand Marais)
Tel. 218-388-2216/800-346-2205 - fax 218-388-9431
- VOYAGER NORTH
(Ely)
Tel. 218-365-3251 - fax 218-365-3251

Missouri
- AKERS FERRY CANOE RENTAL
(Salem)
Tel. 573-858-3224 - fax 573-858-3341
- NORTH FORK RIVER OUTFITTERS
(Dora)
Tel. 417-261-2259

Mississippi
- BLACK CREEK CANOE RENTALS
(Brooklyn)
Tel. 601-582-8817

Montana
- GREAT NORTHERN WHITEWATER
(West Glacier)
Tel. 406-387-5340 - fax 406-387-9007
- MISSOURI RIVER CANOE CO
(Loma)
Tel. 406-378-3110/800-426-2926

Nebraska
- DRYLAND AQUATICS, INC
(Sparks)
Tel. 402-376-3119/800-337-3119

New Hampshire
- SACO VALLEY CANOE
(Center Conway)
Tel. 603-447-2444 - fax 603-447-3280

New Jersey
- JERSEY PADDLER, INC
(Brick)
Tel. 908-458-5777 - fax 908-458-5666
- PINELAND CANOES, INC
(Jackson)
Tel. 908-364-0389

New Mexico
- SAN JUAN CANOE-COMPANY
(Farmington)
Tel. 505-296-7632

New York
- BATTENKILL SPORTSQUARTERS
(Cambridge)
Tel. & fax 518-677-8868
- BAY CREEK PADDLING CENTER
(Rochester)
Tel. 716-288-2830

North Carolina
- NEW RIVER OUTFITTERS
(Jefferson)
Tel. 910-982-9192/800-982-9190 - fax. 910-982-9193
- SOUTHERN WATERWAYS
(Weaverville)
Tel. 704-665-1970

Ohio
- LOUDONVILLE CANOE RENTALS, INC
(Loudonville)
Tel. 419-994-4161/800-226-6356 - fax 419-994-1050
- RIVERS EDGE OUTFITTERS
(Waynesville)
TEL. 973-862-4540

Oklahoma
- SPARROW HAWK
(Tahlequah)
Tel. 918-456-8371/800-722-9635

Oregon
- FREE FLOW WATER TOURS
(Bend)
Tel. 805-772-4302

Pennsylvania
- D & L WATERCRAFTS, INC
(Perkasie)
Tel. 215-453-1818
- OHIOPYLE RAFT RENTAL, INC
(Ohiopyle)
Tel. 800-245-4090 - fax 412-329-4730

South Carolina
- BLACK RIVER EXPEDITIONS
(Georgetown)
Tel. 803-546-4840 - fax 803-527-7840

Tennessee
- HIWASSEE SCENIC RIVER OUTFITTERS
(Reliance)
Tel. 423-338-8115 - fax 423-338-1261

Texas
- AUSTIN OUTDOOR GEAR AND GUIDANCE INC
(Austin)
Tel. 512-473-2644 - fax 512-473-2628
- RIO RAFT COMPANY
(Canyon Lake)
Tel. 210-964-3613 - fax 210-964-3620

Utah
- MOKI MAC RIVER EXPEDITIONS
(Salt Lake City)
Tel. 801-268-6667/800-284-7280 - fax 801-262-093

Virginia
- ADVENTURE CHALLENGE
(Richmond)
Tel. 804-276-7600 - fax 804-276-9750
- TIDEWATER ADVENTURES
(Norfolk)
Tel. 757-480-1999

Vermont
- UMIAK OUTDOOR OUTFITTERS
(Stowe)
Tel. 802-253-2317 - fax 802-253-2551

West Virginia
- ACE WHITEWATER & OUTDOOR CENTER
(Oak Hill)
Tel. 800-787-3982 - fax 304-469-3054

Wisconsin
- MECAN RIVER OUTFITTERS
(Princeton)
Tel. 414-295-3439
- WILD RIVER OUTFITTER
(Grantsburg)
Tel. 715-463-2254

Places of civilization and access routes to the continents

Nearly all the great civilizations in the world have had their origins on the banks of rivers, from which they obtained nutrition and knowledge. Religions, cults, wars, exploration, agriculture, and animal husbandry have had the river as a backdrop. Going back even further in time, rivers were winding paths into the heart of continents that represented a mystery and at the same time a challenge to man. Expeditions, journeys into the unknown, took place by land following the tortuous paths etched by these rivers. With the advent of river navigation, these waterways represented very important communication routes into areas that were heavily forested, but at the same time openings for invaders. In Europe, the Vikings in the 12th century made use of them to invade, and from then on the waterways were used increasingly to penetrate the interior of this continent.

THE FIRST EXPEDITIONS

In Africa and Asia the luxurious and insidious vegetation deterred Europeans from exploring the interiors. The rivers in these regions were also considered far from simple to explore. The Zaire River, which is 2,894 miles (4,660 km) long, crosses the heart of Africa, and eventually runs into the Atlantic, has an average volume of 1,412,000 cubic feet (40,000 cubic m) per second and is inferior only to the Amazon River. Joseph Conrad described it as "an immense snake with its head in the sea and its tail hidden in the heart of the continent." It is therefore not surprising that European geographic maps, until 200 years ago, showed only the outline of Africa with very short rivers, which were often the result of imagination, or legend, on the part of cartographers.

THE LAST UNEXPLORED DESTINATIONS

It was not until the expeditions of Livingstone, Stanley, Baker, Burton, and others in the 19th century, up the Congo, the Nile, and the Zambezi that these rivers were mapped along their entire length to their sources. Within the space of a few decades, until the most recent expeditions of rivers in Borneo, all unexplored areas had been mapped and no more regions held any mysteries.

Morphology

The geological formation of rivers follows a uniform model that only changes according to the type and structure of the rocks. Every watercourse that comes down from a mountain proceeds along the path of least resistance down to the valley floor. Rainwater, like meltwater from glaciers, flows along precise paths on the slope, which eventually meet to form brooks, streams, and finally torrents. Every new confluence is a sign of surface erosion drained by the watercourses and an increase in water flow. The more the torrent descends toward the valley, the wilder it becomes, until the terrain becomes flatter causing a sudden slowing down that results in coarse material being deposited in an alluvial fan. Its size, increased by new confluences, is transformed into a majestic river with meanders that wind across the flood plain.

The average flow of a river means that it doesn't take up all the terrain like when there's a flood. For this reason we can distinguish between the drought riverbed, the normal riverbed, and the floodbed. The drought riverbed is the part occupied during dry periods, the normal one is the area occupied most of the time, while the floodbed is that area, usually covered by vegetation, which is occasionally flooded.

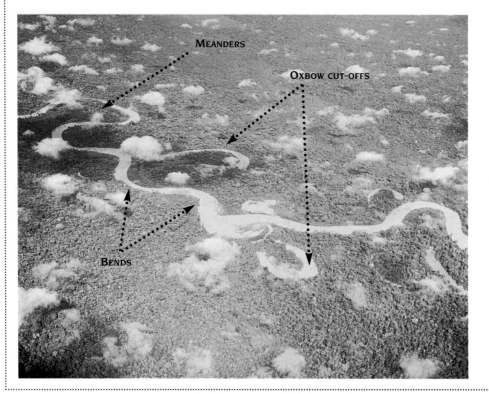

MEANDERS

OXBOW CUT-OFFS

BENDS

BENDS
It's very unusual to see a straight river, because you only need a small vortex or obstacle to start a bend. On the bend of a river, the centrifugal forces push most of the water to the outside, where the speed of the current is greater, causing erosion of the bank, while mud and sand get deposited on the inside of the bend. When the level of water is high, the erosion is faster on the outer bank and the current carries away sand and stones. As a result of the erosion, the outer bend can be deeper, and in the bed there are niches, while on the inner bend, where the current is much weaker, debris and pebbles accumulate causing shallower water.

MEANDERS

Sometimes on a watercourse there is an alternation of very pronounced bends, called meanders, with long, straight parts. Almost all meanders form on the flood plain and owe their origin to banks of hard rocks, which water tends to go around. On the bed of the river the water is forced toward the inside of a meander, bringing with it materials taken from the outside of the bank, whereas the side is convex and the current is not strong enough to carry the suspended material. If the exposed riverbed is not made up of very hard rocks, the meanders tend to "migrate," and over time cause the riverbed to descend toward the valley. All meanders eventually disappear because, when the water level is high, the water tends to skip the bends and take the most direct route.

OXBOW CUT-OFFS

The increase in the bend of a meander can sometimes cause them to become isolated and result in the formation of dead arms. At first the meanders take the form of half-moon canals and are still connected to the river, until gradually the deposits left by the waters cut off all links and only a small lake is left in the form of a scythe which ends up being buried. Oxbow cut-offs are naturally protected areas where fish, insects, and amphibious animals develop in the stagnant water. After a flood, there is usually a limited amount of genetic change.

CATCHMENT BASIN

This is the area where the riverwater and its tributaries collect. The torrents and streams that flow into the main watercourse drain into the watershed, which is indicated by the dashed lines. The Po Basin in Italy covers an area of about 28,958 square miles (75,000 square km), while the Rio basin in the Amazon has a surface area of about 2,7 million square miles (7 million square km). The Colorado River basin covers an area of about 270,270 square miles (700,000 square km).

DESERT WADIS

These are the dried-up beds of old watercourses in the Sahara area, where running water exists only when there is rare local rain. They disappear quickly because of evaporation and the permeability of the riverbed.

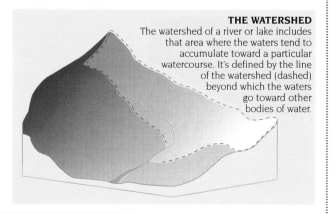

THE WATERSHED

The watershed of a river or lake includes that area where the waters tend to accumulate toward a particular watercourse. It's defined by the line of the watershed (dashed) beyond which the waters go toward other bodies of water.

The river as the creator of the countryside

Running water has been the main agent in transforming the countryside: over time it has excavated the deepest valleys, shaped the most extensive plains, levelled mountains with its erosive action, and filled in depressions with its depositing action. Running water's ability to erode depends on the speed of the water and on the gradient of the river. In the first part of a river, the waters go down a steep slope, loosening and transporting rocky material. Following this the gradients become flatter and the river widens; as the speed of the water decreases near the mouth of the river, the eroded materials are deposited.

On average, all over the world, the erosion rate is about one foot (30 cm) every nine thousand years. If land masses had not risen in the past due to plate tectonics, every relief feature on earth would have been levelled off in 25 million years.

The amount of material that a river can carry increases with its speed. A river on a plain with an average speed is continually transporting sand and gravel, while a torrent with high water is able to transport pebbles inches in diameter.

LINEAR EROSION
Fast and turbulent rivers are able to cut deep valleys creating impressive natural arches and unusually formed cavities in the rocks. Under particular conditions, water can hollow out a cylindrical cavity up to 34 feet (10 m) deep, called a pothole, which is formed by the friction of pebbles moved vortically by the current of the river.

THE ALCANTARA GORGE
In regions where the rock formations are hard, there is little atmospheric erosion and only water erosion plays an important role.

The valleys look more like canyons as can be seen at the Alcantara Gorge in Sicily, where the action of the river has shaped the basaltic rocks

CANYONS

These gorges were cut from a plateau and are characterized by a river running through vertical walls. The Grand Canyon, one of the most impressive examples in the world, is 276 miles (445 km) long, from a mile to 16 miles (1 to 25 km) wide, and nearly 6,560 feet (2,000 m) deep; erosion was started by the Colorado River more than 5 million years ago. The exposed layers of rock are like steps in natural history. At the bottom of the gorge black Precambrian rocks can be seen, some of the oldest on earth. With each successive layer there are impressive changes in color, consistency, and fossil remains in the different formations of limestone and sandstone.

WATERFALLS

They are caused by a sudden and considerable drop in the riverbed. Usually they are formed because of a bank of hard rocks across the valley, which obstruct erosion of the riverbed. The Gulfloss Waterfalls in Iceland, which are famous for the volume of water, are subject to intense erosion, and are receding over time.

DELTAS

They are great alluvial fans that flow into lakes or the sea. Their name is derived from the Greek letter whose shape is similar to that of a delta. If more material is deposited by the river than eroded by the sea, then finger deltas are formed; if the forces are equal, then triangular deltas are formed. Often, as happens in the Mississippi River Delta, the structure can be very complex because of the overlapping of small deltas of different shapes.

Wild and scenic rivers

About 68,000 dams and artificial barriers in the United States have flooded up to 15 percent of the 600,000 miles (960,000 km) of rivers that once flowed freely. Only 149 miles (240 km) of the Missouri River, out of 19,189 miles (3,900 km), is not artificially controlled. On the Colorado River, in the last 30 years not even one molecule of water has reached its estuary. The beautiful upper stretch of the Dolores River, in Colorado, has been sacrificed for irrigation purposes, even if the price of the water is prohibitive for agricultural use. The Glen Canyon on the Colorado, one of the most spectacular sandstone labyrinths in the world, has been covered by Lake Powell. In spite of all these dams, river runners can still enjoy many stretches of water. In 1968, the Wild and Scenic Rivers Act generated a lot of hope for those attracted by the sparkle and roar of free-running water. Some rivers were classified as "wild," meaning that they were without embanking, pollution, and access roads. Others were classified as "landscape," with important environmental value and without any housing. Other rivers were classified as "recreational" and were suitable for water sports. Initially, eight rivers were protected, but eventually Congress increased this to about 150 others. The positive effects of this initiative can be added to that of other protected areas. It seems that the public is aware that there is a need for free waters to protect many life forms, and to maintain the link between man and his natural environment.

TO KNOW THE RIVERS
In order to protect rivers it is essential to know them. These natural environments that are so common to all types of landscapes are not really known well. When the degradation of a river is great or when its banks have been covered with cement, people are less likely to consider it as a fundamental part of landscape. And so, waterways have slowly become marginal areas where less noble activities have turned their banks into garbage dumps. The presence of river runners on rivers has been helpful in creating a better relationship between man and the river.

24

Man-made waterways

After man learned to live with rivers, he made use of them by learning the necessary laws of physics in order to affect the flow of the waters. For thousands of years dams have been used to prevent flooding and make use of water for irrigation. These modifications have, at times, caused unexpected consequences, because complex ecosystems have been disrupted; one of the most important repercussions has been the increase in flooding.

EMBANKMENTS

They stop high waters from flooding the area around the river, preventing alluvial material from being deposited in urbanized or agricultural areas. At the same time, though, they block the natural raising of the alluvial plain and cause material to be deposited within the riverbeds, which can sometimes lead to catastrophic flooding.

CANALS

Interest in river transport was not only confined to the larger rivers. During medieval times many watercourses were modified to allow navigation. At the same time, work was started to connect the main waterways. In 1177, work was started on the Naviglio Grande to bring the waters of the Ticino River to Milan and by 1270 it was made navigable, thus making it an important waterway for commerce. The Naviglio was used, from the end of the 14th century, to transport marble from Candoglia for the construction of the Duomo Cathedral in Milan. Even today, and especially in central Europe, canals are used to connect many countries such as France, Germany, Belgium, and Holland.

RESERVOIRS

A bow-head dam is placed on a river to regulate flow and divert water to irrigation. Excess water flows over the dam to dissipate energy. The resulting wave at the foot of the dam is extremely dangerous and should be avoided if at all possible. Do not run the dam as shown in this photograph.

DAMS

As well as being used for irrigation or hydroelectric purposes, they are also used for controlling high water levels. A consequence has been the flooding of vast areas and the modification of the equilibrium between erosion and transport. Behind the barrier there is a build-up of sediment, while below it the water and soil become poorer and erosion accelerates. In Egypt this phenomenon has caused the Nile Delta to recede and has had a negative effect on coastal fishing.

SALMON LEAP

Fish, by instinct, go back up rivers for breeding, but once they have been carried downstream by a flood they are not able to go upstream because of the artificial barriers, which are too steep, so long stretches of a river may be without any fauna. Many species, such as eels, have abandoned some areas because they can't make their periodic reproductive journeys. For this reason; in many European countries, when a dam is built, it must have a salmon leap to preserve the fish in the rivers.

Flow, speed, and gradient changes

The flow corresponds to the quantity of water that goes through each section of the river, and generally increases as the river goes further downstream. Together with the gradient change and the conformation of the bed, the flow determines the speed of the river. The average speed of a river increases with the gradient and decreases with the roughness of the riverbed. The increase in speed and the ruggedness cause sudden changes that make the flow very turbulent. Large obstacles on the riverbed cause vortexes, as well as areas of calm water, called eddies. A river rarely flows faster than 10 feet (3 m) per second, about 6 miles (10 km) per hour. A slow river is below 1 foot (0.25 m) per second, and a fast one above 1 $\frac{1}{2}$ feet (0.50 m) per second. Rivers on a plain usually flow at less than 3 feet (1 m) per second. A fast river that starts in the mountains can flow at 6 $\frac{1}{2}$ feet (2 m) per second in normal periods, and 10–13 feet (3–4 m) per second in big water.

RAIN SUPPLY
This supplements the meltwater from glaciers and leads to mixed supplies of water, which reach their peak in the period from March to December. Other rivers are mainly supplied by rainwater and rise during the spring thaw.

GLACIAL SUPPLY
Usually they have a variable supply during the year. Much depends on the type of supply; whether it is from rain, snow, ice, or underground water. Melting glaciers in spring supply mountain rivers until about August, when the freezing level is lower than that of the glacier.

KARST SUPPLY
In karst formations, permeated water forms underground rivers, which come to the surface. Karst formations do not have any surface drainage basins, but there are swallow-holes everywhere and circular holes called dolines.

Some layers of underground water can become trapped by an impermeable layer. The height of the stratum can change depending on the season or the year. On the Euphrates they are higher than the level of the river and water exits from these springs visibly.

FLOODS

As a natural disaster it is one that can cause many deaths all over the world. Severe flooding occurs each year as a result of meteorological conditions, deforestation, intensive agriculture, land reclamation, and building on flood plains.

FLOOD WATERBED

This corresponds to the area, usually covered by vegetation, that is occasionally flooded. The river creates an equilibrium based on its average flow. When there is a flood the balance is broken: the strength of the water increases with its speed; waves become unpredictable, trunks float; and in places where the water is usually stagnant, vortexes and whirlpools form; calm stretches disappear; and visibility decreases. Floods are phenomena that reoccur over periods of 10, 20, 40, or every 100 years, and are predictable if statistics on flows and down flows are studied.

DRY WATERBED

They have an irregular and changing form, which corresponds to the lowest flow or drought. The dry waterbed has some water in it even during the dry season.

Main rivers in the world

The longest river in the world is the Nile at 4,143 miles (6,671 km). The widest is the Amazon with a water flow of 6,354,000 cubic feet (180,000 cubic m) per second and it is responsible for 15 percent of the flowing surface water in the world. The Amazon, Orinoco, Parana, Zaire, Yangtze Kiang, and the Ganges between them transport a quarter of the total watercourses on the planet.

The highest waterfall is the Angel waterfall on the Carrao River, a tributary of the Caroni in Venezuela.

The total drop is 3,211 feet (979 m) with the biggest single drop being 2,647 feet (807 m). The most imposing rapid in Europe is the Gavarnie, in the north of the Central Pyrenees, which are 1,381 feet (421 m) high. The Victoria Falls, on the Zambezi River, are famous both for their width and height, and measure 5,740 feet (1,750 m) and 400 feet (122 m) respectively. Those of Niagara on the U.S./Canadian border are 4,166 feet (1,270 m) wide and 161 feet (49 m) high.

MAIN RIVERS IN THE WORLD

RIVER	CONTINENT	LENGTH MILES (KM)		RIVER	CONTINENT	LENGTH MILES (KM)	
NILE-KAGERA	Africa	4,143	(6,671)	COLUMBIA-SNAKE	North America	1,919	(3,090)
MISSISSIPPI-MISSOURI	North America	3,986	(6,418)	ORINOCO	South America	1,863	(3,000)
AMAZON-UCAYALI	South America	3,900	(6,280)	BRAHMAPUTRA	Asia	1,801	(2,900)
JINSHA JINANG	Asia	3,602	(5,800)	COLORADO	North America	1,801	(2,900)
AMAZON-MARAÑÓN	South America	3,416	(5,500)	SÃO FRANCISCO	South America	1,801	(2,900)
OB-IRTYSH	Asia	3,291	(5,300)	RIO GRANDE	North America	1,798	(2,896)
MISSISSIPPI	North America	3,161	(5,090)	DANUBE	Europe	1,776	(2,860)
MISSOURI	North America	3,012	(4,850)	SYR-DAR'YA	Asia	1,776	(2,860)
HUANG HE	Asia	3,009	(4,845)	EUPHRATES	Asia	1,714	(2,760)
DE LA PLATA-PARANÁ	South America	2,919	(4,700)	GANGES	Asia	1,677	(2,700)
MEKONG	Asia	2,795	(4,500)	ZAMBEZI	Africa	1,652	(2,660)
AMUR-KERULEN	Asia	2,782	(4,480)	TOCANTINS	South America	1,639	(2,640)
LENA	Asia	2,732	(4,400)	ARAGUAIA	South America	1,615	(2,600)
ZAIRE	Africa	2,608	(4,200)	CHURCHILL	North America	1,608	(2,590)
NIGER	Africa	2,583	(4,160)	AMU-DAR'YA	Asia	1,577	(2,540)
MACKENZIE	North America	2,512	(4,045)	NU JIANG	Asia	1,577	(2,540)
OB-KATUN	Asia	2,494	(4,016)	URAL	Europe/Asia	1,574	(2,534)
YENSISEY	Asia	2,364	(3,807)	OLENEK	Asia	1,500	(2,415)
ST. LAWRENCE	North America	2,360	(3,800)	VISTULA	Europe	861	(1,387)
YUKON	North America	2,298	(3,700)	RHINE	Europe	820	(1,320)
VOLGA	Europe	2,193	(3,531)	ELBE	Europe	723	(1,165)
MURRAY-DARLING	Australia	2,167	(3,490)	LOIRE	Europe	628	(1,012)
MADEIRA-MAMORÉ	South America	1,987	(3,200)	RHONE	Europe	504	(812)
PURUS	South America	1,987	(3,200)	SEINE	Europe	482	(776)
INDUS	Asia	1,975	(3,180)	GARONNA	Europe	419	(674)
NELSON-SASKATCHEWAN	North America	1,969	(3,170)	PO	Europe	405	(652)

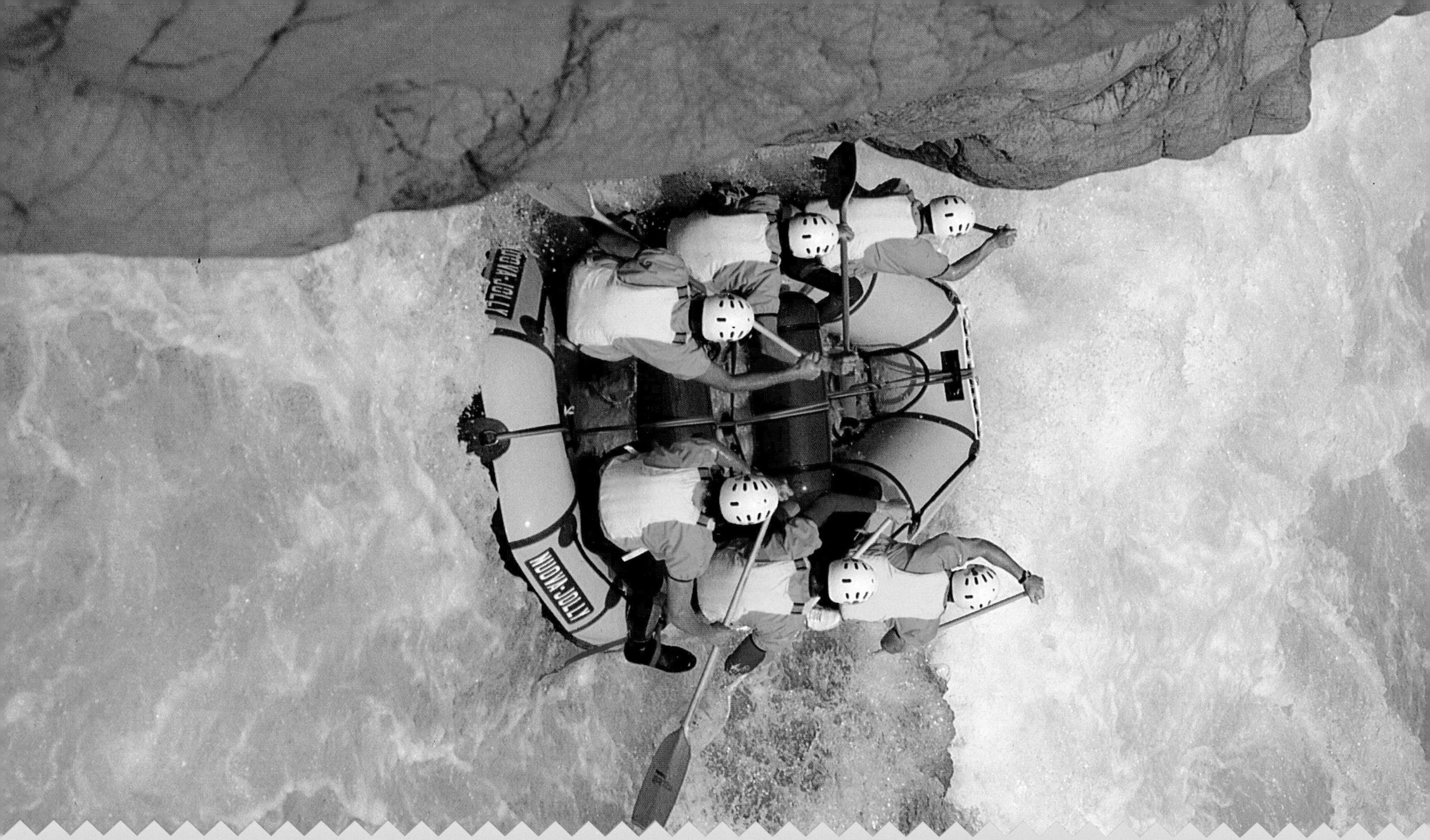

SPORTS RIVER RUNS

The search for the ideal run

If we plan the descent of a river that is frequently visited or one of the classics, then it's very easy to obtain material at specialized book shops. If, on the other hand, we wish to go on one of the less frequented rivers it's better to ask one of the local guides to find out about difficulties.

Some rivers, though, lie in remote regions or can be run only for short periods during the year and therefore information is scarce. The essential things to establish before a run are the flow, the state and gradient of the riverbed, and the presence of natural or artificial obstacles such as dams or pressurized water pipes. To be able to do an exciting run there must be an average drop of between 10 and 40 feet per mile, it must not be dry, i.e., a minimum flow of 500-700 cubic feet (15-20 cubic m) per second, nor can there be big water with a flow of more than 750-800 cubic feet (50-60 cubic m) per second. It may happen that having put the inflatable in the water under seemingly ideal conditions, the river becomes dry and the raft must be portaged for several miles to get around an obstacle. A much worse situation is when the raft is put into big water, or when it is about to happen. To avoid any risks, some precise signs to look for are water that is muddied by the transport of sand and current that is pulling along branches and other objects from further upstream.

PLANNING A RUN

By examining a map, the height of the put-in and take-out can be noted, and from there the drop of the run can be calculated. Some knowledge of the geography of the area is necessary because the drop could be concentrated in one waterfall. When doing a run for the first time, it's a good idea to find out precise information about the put-in and take-out, to know the exact distance that separates them and, therefore, the time needed to do the run. It should be remembered that a raft travels at a speed of about 6.2 miles (10 km) per hour but this could increase if portaging is necessary. It's better to establish a departure time so that when night falls the raft is not still on the river, and you should also know where it's possible to organize safety and rescue maneuvers.

Classification of difficulties

In Europe a standard system has been adopted to rate the difficulty of a river. This system is valid for both rafts and kayaks and is divided into six different classes, which are described on page 42. In the southwestern United States another system known as the Desert Scale or Grand Canyon System is used. It grades rivers between 10 and 10+.

Class I

Class II

Class III

Class IV

Class V

Class VI

The river as a playing field

Whoever decides to run a river knows that a particular point of view has been chosen; you become small and observe from below, with slow movements: a watercourse is measured in days and weeks. When you are navigating a boat, your relationship with nature is not passive. Soon you learn that the river has its own laws, both natural and external. A cubic foot of water weighs 62 pounds, and a small river can transport 350 cubic feet per second. Experience teaches you to forsee obstacles and difficulties and to use the right maneuvers for every event, relying on your intelligence and the harmony within the group. Because of the freedom it allows, the greatest attraction of rafting is in the exploration and the adventure on the river, rather than merely the athletic aspect of the sport.

THE CAMPSITE
This is often an integral part of a weekend's rafting. Clubs frequently offer this possibility to the runners.

Spending a night in a tent or in a hammock near a rapid can be relaxing or cause insomnia, but never indifference.

GROUPS
They discover a mutual understanding during the preparation course and the run.

KNOWLEDGE OF THE RIVER ENVIRONMENT
Knowledge gained from running a river is different from that gained from walking along its banks. The river is alive, and learning to understand it can be a very fulfilling experience.

CHALLENGING YOUR OWN LIMITS
This is one of the main reasons for running a rapid. Fear, emotion, and satisfaction at having faced an unusual situation are all common feelings during this experience.

Big rapids

After having done the first river run, there is certainly the desire to try a more challenging run during which your emotional involvement is extraordinary. In the most turbulent parts of a river, the violence of the hydraulics and the feeling of being at the complete mercy of a natural element is very strong. Approaching a big rapid, first you hear the thunder of the water, then you watch as the river disappears in front of the inflatable because of the drop. The speed and the noise increase as you get nearer to the drop, until you feel the first waves starting to jolt the raft. The biggest waves, with their breakers, can submerge the whole crew, so each runner has to be careful to hold tightly.

THE GUIDE
He must remain calm and take into account that some of the crew may not be able to paddle because they have to hold on to the handles. During the run, some of the inexperienced runners may feel very strong emotions. Some people scream out loud while others remain perfectly still, hardly breathing. The guide must reassure and keep the crew under control. On very long rapids, when the inflatable fills up with water and becomes difficult to maneuver, it's up to the guide to keep it on course.

IMPRACTICAL RUNS
It is not always possible to run a rapid with an inflatable. When the river becomes very narrow or there is a high waterfall, the raft can be too bulky and it's better to run the rapid with something lighter, like a kayak.

IMPORTANT RIVERS
The rapids on the most popular rivers all have a name. The run on the Colorado River starts at the Badger Creek Rapid and finishes at the Emery Falls, going through Horn Creek Rapid and the Lava Falls. The latter is one of the most demanding where even the biggest rafts risk capsizing.

Extreme runs

Some people are more interested in looking for the thrill of whitewater, rather than for naturalistic or sports reasons. The first rafters to run the Rio Calco Canyon, in Peru, and the Class V rapids that extend for tens of miles on the Urubamba River, also in Peru, were pushing themselves to the limit of highest risk; even though there had been previous expeditions, it was not possible to forsee what sort of situation would be encountered. Nevertheless, the first run on an extreme descent always creates an element of mystery and tension for the crew of an inflatable. On all rapids above Class V difficulty, the raft is continually subject to jolting by the force of the water, the gradient difference, and the speed at which natural obstacles are passed. This creates a situation where the crew is not always in complete control of the raft. There comes the moment when the crew must be daring: once you have entered the rapid there is no turning back.

Whoever wants to run the most violent rapids will find them all over the world: The Livingstone Falls on the Zaire River, The Lava Falls on the Colorado River, the Frazer Rapids in Canada, the Bio Bio Rapids in Chile, the rapids on the Himalayan rivers, and the famous ones on the Yang Tze in China.

RAPIDS IN EUROPE
The most famous
rapids in Europe are the
Inn gorge in Austria,
the rapids on the
Otzaler Ache, in the
Tyrol, Austria, and
the Class V on the
Ubay in France.

Portaging

High waterfalls, siphons created by broken boulders in the river, and tree trunks can block an inflatable, making it necessary to portage, which can be long, tiring, and complicated. For example, on the Marsyangdi River in Nepal, at a certain point the river disappears underground for a few miles, making a daylong portage obligatory. The most impractical areas are those where the morphology is the most uneven, forcing the rafter to climb, often lowering the inflatable into the water using ropes. Portaging becomes even more complicated when the raft has to be emptied; the banks are often slippery and dangerous, because frequently the rocks on a waterfall are craggy.

CHOICE OF A SUITABLE PLACE
In such circumstances, it is the guide who must decide where to do the portage, as well as give precise instructions to the crew on what to do.

ABANDONING THE INFLATABLE
The rapids on which the Zambezi reaches the lake below, where the classic run finishes, are extremely dangerous. The enormous mass of water flows into a very narrow passage only several feet wide, and irregular vortexes are created that tend to suck up any objects, even bulky ones. This means that if a rafter falls overboard he risks being pulled to the bottom with fatal consequences. For this reason, organizers of runs down the Zambezi opt for a portage on foot by the passengers, while the empty inflatable with the oars and load securely tied goes down this stretch of the rapid and is recovered from the lake below.

The scale of river difficulty – six classes

The scale of difficulty of a river is divided into six very synthetic and easily-used classes. The classes, however, are not able to give an exhaustive description of a river, because an increase in the flow can change the difficulty from one moment to the next. Impor-tant changes to the riverbed can also happen afte[r] a flood. During a run the crew of an inflatable can com[e] across unforseen obstacles such as metal cables, a[r]tificial interventions made by an excavator, or eve[n] trunks that have blocked the watercourse.

CLASS I

EASY. Open spaces. The run is regular. Any waves or breakers are limited in size. If there are any obstacles they are obvious and easily missed.

CLASS II

NOT VERY DIFFICULT. The river is almost completely free of rocks and other obstacles, and the water is quite fast-moving. There are some straightforward rapids with small waves and simple breakers. Some maneuvering may be necessary. Rocks are clearly visible and the gradient is not excessive. Risks to swimmers are small but knowledge of simple self-rescue techniques and swimming in a current is useful.

CLASS III

AVERAGE DIFFICULTY. The river may be quite demanding, with bends that obscure views of the rapids. There is a fairly steep gradient, with rocks in the current and small drops. Tight bends and strainers may be present. There are breakers and high and irregular waves.

CLASS IV

DIFFICULT. The route is not very visible in advance and there are big, continuous waves with strong rollers. There are rocks in the main current with drops, and holes with a backwash, together with restricted and obligatory passages. It is necessary from this class up to have a thorough knowledge of rescue techniques, because some rollers can flip over an inflatable and rocks could cause a wrap.

CLASS V

VERY DIFFICULT. It is a run only for expert paddlers who must scout the river before descending. The rapids are violent and may contain large, unavoidable waves. There are keeper holes and the chutes and waterfalls have difficult entries and exits. It is preferable to descend only if precautions have been taken for eventual rescue.

CLASS VI

EXTREME. There are a succession of jumps with keeper holes, siphons, possible wraps, and violent backwashes. The mass and speed of the water makes controlling the raft difficult. Detailed scouting is necessary and the dangers must be weighed carefully. Because of the risks, a rescue team must be present on the river bank.

Canoeing

The open canoe was originally used by Native Americans to move about on the rivers and lakes in the North. They were built from a wooden structure that was curved while hot, and then covered with birch and sewed with roots, and finally waterproofed using pine resin. Following colonization, between the 17th and 19th centuries, different materials were used for construction. As a result of more sophisticated techniques, an internal structure with ribs covered with thin, nailed-on strips started to be used.

After this the canoes were lightened by usi[ng] a covering of waterproofed canvas, which n[ow] has been replaced by fiberglass. Aluminu[m] models were very popular in the United States [be]cause they were light and easy to repair, but eve[n]tually fiberglass – on its own or mixed wi[th] other synthetic materials, such as kevlar, th[at] strengthen and lighten at the same time – ha[s] been used.

Portaging
The traditional canoe is perhaps the most refined way to navigate on a river, not only because it still maintains the shape and techniques used in the past, but also because it allows a simple and immediate approach to places that have maintained their original beauty. As well as being a fast means, it's easily maneuvered, silent, sturdy, and easy to carry on your shoulders.

Competitions
There are also freestyle and slalom competitions for the traditional canoes. The main difference is that they are covered and built with different principles so that they a[re] lighter and have other functional specifications[.]

Rapids in a canoe
In a canoe they should only be tried after some experience in whitewater. Whereas in a raft it's possible to run rapids without any preparation, a canoeist must possess the technical skills to be able [to] control the canoe very wel[l]

Kayaking

In spite of its Eskimo origins, and almost certainly marine, the kayak has shown itself to be ideal in getting over the difficulties of river navigation. It's a covered canoe, about 6 to 13 feet (2 to 4 m) long, and pushed by a double-bladed paddle. On wider rivers, the shape is more flared around the middle and the decks are narrower, while on torrents with sharp drops the decks are stronger and are much more buoyant. Because of its great versatility, canoeists have a better knowledge the geography of runs, of maneuvers in whit water, and safety techniques. They were the fir at the beginning of the sixties, to explore t network of rivers in Europe and in many other pa of the world, acting as the predecessors of t rafters.

RALLIES
Reunions of canoeists happen every year on the most famous and interesting rivers. The real enthusiasts, who are always on the lookout for new runs, make the most of these occasions to meet up with others.

COMPETITIONS
Most of the advances in the technique of kayaking is a direct result of modification in competitions to get the best results. The sla has become on of the best-kno and spectacular disciplines in th Olympics.

SUITABLE MEANS FOR RAPIDS
The shortest boats are used on mountain torrents and allow tight turns and the ability to get out of difficult situations easily, such as a series of jumps.

Hydrospeeding

The hydrospeed is a type of river bob invented in France. It's used on rivers and torrents with plenty of water, which are at least Class III or IV, and is very exciting to use. The user lies face down and swims in the whitewater with his body partially immersed in the water, wearing flippers, and holds on tightly to the hydrospeed, which floats and protects the body like a shield. The view of the river is very different from that of other watercrafts because the eyes are at water level; the view is limited, and the tactile sensitivity of the body

is more important. What makes river running with a hydrospeed unique is the total contact with the river currents.

Various models exist on the market, but they are usually made from polyethylene and filled with polyurethane foam. Their volume ranges from 50 to 80 liters. The handholds, made of aluminium, are located in a space that protects the forearms and elbows. The inflatable version, called "hydrosac" by the French, is lighter and less stable and looks like a backpack.

OBSTACLES

When there are obstacles, it is advisable to hold on tightly to prevent the hydrospeed from being ripped from under you; if this happens the runner is without any protection and is at the mercy of the current and hindered by the flippers. To increase stability, widen the legs. If you get knocked over, do an eskimo quickly, i.e., right yourself by flapping the flippers and quickly moving the forearms at the same time.

CLOTHING

To do hydrospeeding it is necessary to wear a special life vest, a specially reinforced wet suit, a canoeing helmet with a chin strap, and flippers over booties. The longer runs are made more comfortable by use of gloves and a neoprene cap. A mask and snorkel are only used for the most violent runs, because besides obstructing the view, the high and frequent waves make it difficult to breathe easily.

SAFETY

To descend safely, it's best to do so in groups with a rope and safety harness for every two or three people. Scouting of the more demanding stretches can highlight any submerged obstacles. For longer runs, it's a good idea to be accompanied by a raft or other craft

TECHNIQUES
The run is started by carefully entering the water and then using flippers to propel the hydrospeed. It's important to reach the main current quickly, where the water is deeper and faster. To go in the direction wanted you only go across the current. To turn you need to flap the flippers sideways, and incline your pelvis. The only way to stop is to reach an eddy downstream of rocks near the bank.

Canyoning

Until several decades ago, gorges were only explored by speleologists. Then canoeists and climbers started looking for new challenges and tried the emotion of moving between waterfalls and chutes, crossing enormous potholes, canyons, and underground siphons. These activities were developed in places like France and Spain, where the new sport started. A gorge or a ravine is descended by walking in the water or even crawling, climbing rocks, descending on a single or double rope, sliding, diving, or swimming.

GETTING OVER WATERFALLS

The smallest waterfalls can be descended on foot or even, in a more playful way, by sliding down them, holding your elbows in front of the stomach, on your back. The highest waterfalls can be descended by using a double rope, which is not so difficult, but is complicated by the effect of the water pressure on your head.

EQUIPMENT NEEDED

Essentials are a sleeveless wet suit, a neoprene jacket, heavy-duty overalls, gloves and hood, isothermal shoes and booties, life vest, and backpack. To go down gorges and to climb waterfalls basic climbing gear is needed. Every group must have a first aid kit, an aluminium blanket, matches, and a head torch for unexpected overnight stays.

THE WATERWAY

The first rule of canyoning is to follow the river. Going along the canyon bottom many demanding situations are met: waterfalls, blind bends, oblique slides, narrow parts, stretches to be done underwater. All these make it necessary to have a good knowledge of climbing techniques, the use of ropes, and speleological maneuvers.

Club listings

Alabama
- LOCUST FORK RACING ORGANIZATION
(Rainbow City)
Tel. 205-442-1345

Alaska
- KNIK CANOERS KAYAKERS
(Anchorage)
Tel. 907-272-9351

Arizona
- PRESCOTT PADDLE AMERICA CLUB
(Prescott)
Tel. 520-445-5480
- SOUTHERN ARIZONA PADDLERS CLUB
(Tucson)
Tel. 602-327-5717

Arkansas
- ARKANSAS CANOE CLUB
(Little Rock)
Tel. 501-321-8589

California
- BAY AREA SEA KAYAKERS
(San Rafael)
Tel. 415-457-6094
- CALIFORNIA NATIONAL CANOE CLUB
(Clovis)
Tel. 209-322-1406
- SANTA CRUZ KAYAK CLUB
(Santa Cruz)
Tel. 408-458-1080
- SIX RIVERS PADDLING CLUB
(Arcata)
Tel. 707-822-4602

Colorado
- ASPEN KAYAK SCHOOL
(Aspen)
Tel. 970-925-6248
- COLORADO WHITEWATER ASSOCIATION
(Boulder)
Tel. 303-447-0068
- ROCKY MOUNTAIN CANOE CLUB
(Lakewood)
Tel. 303-987-8112

Connecticut
- COLUMBIA CANOE CLUB
(Mansfield)
Tel. 203-456-4906
- CONNECTICUT CANOE RACING
ASSOCIATION
(East Hartford)
Tel. 203-289-0015

Delaware
- WILMINGTON TRAIL CLUB
(Wilmington)
Tel. 302-368-5533

Florida
- EMERALD COAST PADDLERS
(Valparaiso)
Tel. 904-678-4159
- FLORIDA CANOE & KAYAK ASSOCIATION
(West Palm Beach)
Tel. 407-686-8800
- WEST FLORIDA CANOE CLUB
(Pensacola)
Tel. 904-453-3298

Georgia
- ATLANTA WHITEWATER CLUB
(Clarkston)
Tel. 404-299-3752
- GEORGIA CANOEING ASSOCIATION
(Atlanta)
Tel. 404-266-3734

Hawaii
- HAWAIIAN SAILING CANOE ASSOCIATION
(Kaunakakai)
Tel. 808-558-8367
- HEALANI CANOE CLUB
(Honolulu)
Tel. 808-599-3996

Idaho
- IDAHO RIVER SPORTS CANOE CLUB
(Boise)
Tel. 208-336-4844

Illinois
- CHICAGO WHITEWATER ASSOCIATION
(Schaumburg)
Tel. 708-213-8810
- PRAIRIE STATE CANOEISTS
(Downers Grove)
Tel. 815-634-2811

Indiana
- HOOSIER CANOE CLUB
(Noblesville)
Tel. 317-773-6216

Iowa
- MIDWEST RIVER EXPEDITIONS
(Dubuque)
Tel. 319-556-7518

Kansas
- KANSAS CANOE ASSOCIATION
(Wichita)
Tel. 316-662-0346

Kentucky
- VIKING CANOE CLUB
(Louisville)
Tel. 502-459-4881

Louisiana
- BOUNDARY WATERS ADVENTURE
ASSOCIATION
(Leesville)
Tel. 318-238-0821

Maine
- PENOBSCOT PADDLE & CHOWDER
(Brewer)
Tel. 207-989-3878

Maryland
- ALLEVA TRIPPING CLUB
(Darnestown)
Tel. 301-417-2994
- AMERICAN WHITEWATER AFFILIATION
(Silver Spring)
Tel. 301-236-0436
- POTOMAC RIVER PADDLERS
(Germantown)
Tel. 301-353-9237

Massachussetts
- BOSTON SEA KAYAK CLUB
(Beverly)
Tel. 607-631-8640

Michigan
- GREAT LAKES PADDLERS
(Ypsilanti)
Tel. 313-481-1883
- WEST MICHIGAN COASTAL
KAYAKER'S ASSOCIATION
(Grand Rapids)
Tel. 616-331-2558

Minnesota
- MINNESOTA CANOE ASSOCIATION
(Minneapolis)
Tel. 612-985-1111

Missouri
- MISSOURI WHITEWATER ASSOCIATION
(St. Louis)
Tel. 314-727-2213

Montana
- FLATHEAD WHITEWATER ASSOCIATION
(Whitefish)
Tel. 406-862-2386

New Hampshire
- LEDYARD CANOE CLUB
(Hanover)
Tel. 603-643-6709

Nevada
- SIERRA NEVADA WHITEWATER CLUB
(Reno)
Tel. 702-787-1751

New Jersey
- GARDEN STATE CANOE CLUB
(Millington)
Tel. 908-382-6877
- KAYAK & CANOE CLUB-NEW YORK
(Kinnelon)
Tel. 914-688-5569

New Mexico
- ADOBE WHITEWATER CLUB
(Albuquerque)
Tel. 505-296-6586

New York
- APPALACHIAN MOUNTAIN CLUB
(Wingdale)
Tel. 914-832-6575
- DOWNTOWN BOAT CLUB
(New York)
Tel. 212-966-1852
- NISSEQUOGUE RIVER CANOE CLUB
(Huntington)
Tel. 516-679-1362
- ZOAR VALLEY PADDLERS CLUB
(Buffalo)
Tel. 716-592-7497

North Carolina
- WESTERN CAROLINA PADDLERS
(Asheville)
Tel. 704-251-6552

Ohio
- DAYTON CANOE CLUB
(Dayton)
Tel. 513-222-9392

Oklahoma
- ARKANSAS CANOE CLUB
(Tulsa)
Tel. 918-742-1319

Oregon
- NORTHWEST RAFTERS ASSOCIATION
(Portland)
Tel. 503-246-0386
- OREGON CANOE RACING
ASSOCIATION
(Oregon City)
Tel. 503-681-9023

Pennsylvania
- FOOTHILLS PADDLING CLUB
(Greenville)
Tel. 803-268-7275

Rhode Island
- RHODE ISLAND CANOE ASSOCIATION
(Pawtucket)
Tel. 401-725-3344

South Carolina
- COASTAL CANOE AND KAYAK CLUB
(N. Myrtle Beach)
Tel. 803-272-4420

Tennessee
- UNIVERSITY OF TENNESSEE CANOE
AND HIKING CLUB
(Knoxville)
Tel. 615-974-5178

Texas
- ALAMO CITY RIVERMEN
(San Antonio)
Tel. 512-641-0548
- NORTH TEXAS RIVER RUNNERS
(Bedford)
Tel. 817-468-8832

Utah
- UTAH WHITEWATER CLUB
(Salt Lake City)
Tel. 801-355-4126/801-466-5141

Vermont
- VERMONT PADDLERS CLUB
(Essex Junction)
Tel. 802-878-6828

Virginia
- CANOE CRUISERS ASSOCIATION
(Arlington)
Tel.703-532-7881
- COASTAL CANOEISTS
(Richmond)
Tel. 804-231-0118

Washington
- NORTHWEST WHITEWATER
ASSOCIATION
(Spokane)
Tel. 509-299-2777
- WASHINGTON KAYAK CLUB
(Seattle)
Tel. 206-271-7655

West Virginia
- WEST VIRGINIA WHITEWATER
ASSOCIATION
(South Charleston)
Tel. 304-744-0878

Wisconsin
- HOOFERS OUTING CLUB
(Madison)
Tel. 608-258-1699

Wyoming
- JACKSON HOLE KAYAK CLUB
(Jackson)
Tel. 307-733-2471

The raft

The raft is made up of a series of tubular air chambers, so that if one of them is punctured, only that one deflates. It's impossible to sink, and is relatively light and floats in such a way that allows any type of maneuver on the surface of waves. Because it has no rigid parts and continuous sides, it is able to absorb knocks by stones at any point. Because the floor is so wide and flat, it's very stable, but this does not mean that it can always cope with very high waves, especially if the weig[ht] of the crew is not well distributed. The raft has [a] symmetrical shape with the two decks being mo[re] or less the same. The smallest models, which ca[n] transport three or four people, are no more tha[n] 10 feet (3m) long, while those for 6 to 10 peopl[e] which are more frequently used, are fro[m] 13 to 16 feet (4 to 5) long and weigh about 1[?] pounds (60 kg).

FLOORS
This is the most important part of the raft. The first rafts had flat floors, made by joining tubes by means of a simple rubberized canvas. Water that accumulated quickly in the raft could not escape, and the raft became a sort of floating bath – very heavy and difficult to manage – and the crew was forced to bail out the water. Even though these rafts were replaced by ones with self-bailing floors, they are still used on rapids like on the Colorado and the Sun Kosi, because as they fill with water and become heavier, they're more stable.

MATERIAL
The material used to make the rafts is exactly the same as that used to make inflatable marine boats. It's usually made of a base fabric covered with a waterproof material such as neoprene or hypalon. The outer layer, besides being

waterproof, must also be resistant to the sun and rock abrasion.

SELF-BAILING FLOORS
They are made from the same material as the rafts, and laid out in such a way that they form an air chamber about 8 inches (20 cm) thick. This structure is fixed to the rest of the raft by special tabs or rings. The volume of the self-bailing floor means that it floats better and can support th[e] raft and its entire load. It[s] main defect is its cost an[d] the fact that the openings while letting water out, also inevitably let some water in, meaning the crew navigates with wet feet.

VALVES

They do not seem so important, but the reliability of a raft depends on them. Each air chamber has a valve, which must be easily reached and allow quick deflation. Special safety valves can also be fitted, like those on pressure cookers, to let out excess air during inflation or when there's excess pressure if the raft has been exposed to the sun for a long period.

FOOT-STRAPS

They are perhaps the most important accessory for safety and must be correctly positioned. In whitewater the raft is jolted about. To avoid falling overboard while paddling, these straps on the floor are used.

ANCHORAGE RINGS

They are fixed to the bow and stern, and can resist the traction of the raft submerged in the current. They are used in rescue maneuvers, and also when the raft is anchored on the bank with a cord.

The cataraft

A cataraft consists of two tubes attached with a rigid aluminium frame, which is very light and maneuverable, as well as simple and easy to build. Because they are faster than traditional inflatables, catarafts are more suited for races but are less suitable for recreational use, as they offer less protection to the crew and the position on them is more uncomfortable. Also, if one of the air chambers deflates and sinks, then the whole structure can hit the riverbed. In this case, the inflatable risks getting stuck, and it could be difficult to recover it. The aluminium tubes could also be dangerous to the rafter if there is a collision.

STRAPS
The most difficult problem for a cataraft crew is the position on board; the rafter must use support straps, which are not necessary on a normal inflatable.

Often the rafters sit astride the tubes, but this position can be very dangerous when, in rapids, there are rocks or other obstacles difficult to avoid.

RACES
Crews build their own craft, which are not normally found in commercial shops. This has led to numerous

handmade prototypes, which in turn has resulted in improvements in the hydrodynamic characteristics and weight of these craft.

IN RUSSIA
River running in catarafts is such a popular sport in Russia that thousands of people can be seen at races and rallies.

The inflatable canoe

On smaller rivers, where a normal inflatable would not be able to pass, an inflatable canoe, which is halfway between a raft and a kayak, shows how agile and maneuverable it is. Although it's not so big, it's able to carry quite large loads, as its buoyancy is about the same as other inflatables. The materials and techniques used in its construction are more or less the same as for bigger rafts, but when deflated it can go into a bag which can be carried like a backpack. It is therefore very practical to use where there are no access roads or where frequent portages are necessary.

PRIVATE USE
Anyone can buy an inflatable canoe and organize a river run either alone or with one or two people. With a raft, the cost, the problem of transport and recovery, and the problem of getting together a group of people means that it is not used much by private individuals.

THE INDIAN CANOE
In some cases the builders of these craft tend to imitate the shape of the traditional Indian canoe.

RACES
For these small craft, competitions for two-person crews are held.

TECHNIQUES
An inflatable canoe can run almost the same rapids as a raft. Because it is narrower and therefore less stable, a better knowledge of techniques is necessary, as in some particularly turbulent situations it could flip over.

RESTRICTED SPACES
Unlike a raft, which needs a good level of water, these canoes can run rivers with a very narrow riverbed.

PADDLING
The paddling position is quite comfortable in an inflatable canoe.

MANEUVERS BETWEEN ROCKS
The shorter versions are for use where torrents allow tight maneuvers and permit getting out of difficult passages such as a succession of jumps.

Equipment and clothing

Submersion in freezing cold water for long periods leads to loss of body heat and can have serious consequences; it leads to slower reactions and potentially dangerous situations. For this reason, anyone practising river sports should always wear an insulated wet suit and other warm clothing. All accessories should be comfortable to wear, of good quality, and in good condition. Plastic materials should be exposed to the sun as little as possible.

WET SUITS

They should be made of fleece-lined 3-millimeter neoprene and cover the legs and chest, leaving the shoulders and arms free. It is advisable to wear woolen clothing under the wet suit, which absorbs sweat and keeps body temperature constant. Besides keeping out the cold and being buoyant, the wet suit helps protect against any knocks. Places where there might be more wear and tear should be protected with neoprene patches.

DRY SUITS

For winter runs in the northern and mountain states, there are special dry suits made from PVC, neoprene, or Gore-tex. They have special tight-fitting latex gaskets, and a special waterproof zipper that prevents water from getting in.

HELMETS

It is essential not only in case someone falls overboard but also to protect the head from tree branches and possible collisions with other river runners. Helmets specifically for river sports, either light or rigid, offer complete protection for the forehead and the cheeks.

LIFE VESTS

Following modern ideas about safety, a life vest is used to keep a person afloat with the head above the water, even when the person is unconscious. Besides offering quite good protection from blows, they must not hinder movement in whitewater and must have a quick release system. When choosing a life vest, it's better to get one with a bright color that is clearly visible under water. It should also be Type III Coast Guard—approved.

THROW BAGS

This contains about 60 feet of $\frac{1}{2}$-inch rope, a carabiner, a pulley, and a knife and completes the personal equipment.

WATERPROOF BAGS

They are essential during a trip to keep clothes, provisions and photographic equipment dry. They are made from lined materials and some have two straps so they can be carried on the back.

Inflation and maintenance

The ideal pressure for an inflatable raft is 0.3 atmospheres, but it is up to the individual rafter to decide, depending on the performance he wants. On particularly violent rapids it's better if the raft is slightly under-pressure so that it can absorb rigidly blows better, while in other circumstances, when it's preferable to go quickly past obstacles, it's better to have the raft inflated as rigidly as possible. Once the raft is inflated, it's directly subject to atmospheric conditions. If it's left out overnight or used on an ice-cold river, the gas pressure will be less and it will be less inflated. If it's left in the sun the gas will expand. At very high temperatures it could even explode.

Pumps

They are used to inflate the raft and can be of three types: manual, foot, or electric. The electric pump that runs at 12 volts, and can be connected to a car battery, is the most convenient, but also the most expensive and possibly the most delicate. The foot pump is the most widely-used, while the hand pump, which takes up little space, is good to have on board if greater pressure is needed. Before using it, make sure it's dry to avoid the risk of water in the air chambers.

MANUAL PISTON PUMP

FOOT PUMP

THWARTS
These are inserted once the raft has been inflated and help to strengthen it. The bigger rafts may need three or four of these.

VACUUM CLEANERS
An ordinary domestic vacuum cleaner with the exhaust tube attached to the raft valve can be used to inflate the raft. To finish the job off, a double action pump can be used to get the right pressure.

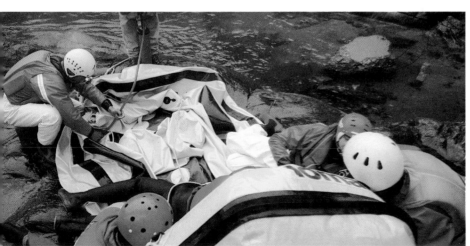

REPAIRS
It's possible that the raft will hit a stone or sharp object violently during a run. When an air chamber is cut, it deflates quickly and fills up with water; but as the raft is made up of separate air chambers, the entire structure loses maneuverability and gets heavier. To repair a cut, the raft first needs to be completely dry. Then take a patch of the same material, sand the damaged part, apply a rubberized glue on the patch and on the raft and wait for about ten minutes. Apply the patch and press hard to eliminate any air bubbles. For more serious damage, such as the seams coming apart or lacerations, it is advisable to contact the raft builder.

Anatomy of the raft

Through experience of river running, it's now considered better to have inflatables with a symmetrical shape, with the bow and stern more or less the same shape. Good stability and steering is obtained, regardless of the size, by having the length about twice as long as the width. The continuous profile has a constant diameter and is proportional to the size of the inflatable. However, even on the biggest rafts it's preferable not to exceed 24 inches (60 cm) so that the center of gravity is not affected excessively, the internal space of the raft is reduced, and above all to make it easier for the paddlers to work. If a paddler sits too far from the water surface, it becomes difficult to paddle effectively.

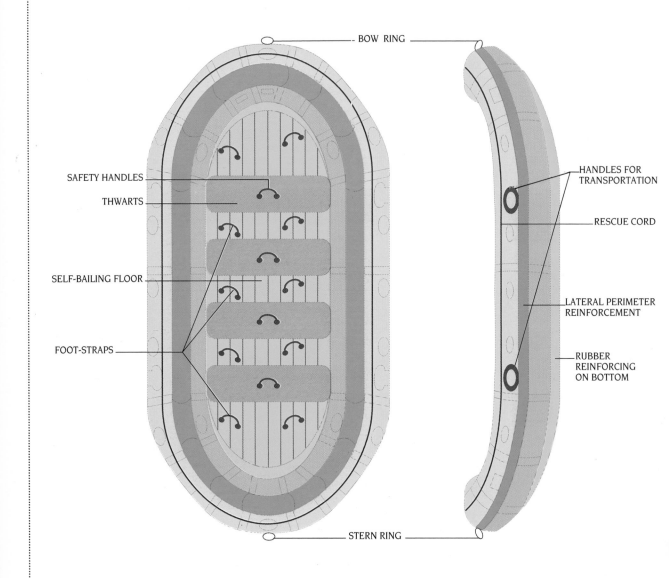

BOW RING

SAFETY HANDLES

THWARTS

SELF-BAILING FLOOR

FOOT-STRAPS

STERN RING

HANDLES FOR TRANSPORTATION

RESCUE CORD

LATERAL PERIMETER REINFORCEMENT

RUBBER REINFORCING ON BOTTOM

RACES AND TOURIST RUNS

Rallies

Rallies are one of the most spectacular and picturesque ways for coming into contact with the world of rafting. The participants often bring along their families and friends, and the site and the river soon fill up with colored inflatables, river runners, and spectators on the river banks getting to know people from all over the world.

These occasions are frequently transformed into a party atmosphere, and in many parts of the world rafting enthusiasts do not hesitate to travel long distances to participate.

ON THE RIVER
Parking lots full of vehicles with inflatables are typical at these events.

COSTA R
Many rallies are held Costa Rica because of t many rivers that, during t rainy season, are full water, and the timi frequently coincides wi international race

BEFORE RACES
Sometimes rallies coincide with an important race and rafters can swap crafts, paddles, and crews

as well as have long, animated discussions about the best route to ta and the dangers and obstacles on the rapids.

Wildwater races

River runners can compete in exciting races. The team that manages to do the run in the fastest time is the winner. The races can be of various lengths. If on a short race of several hundred yards there are difficult rapids, it's known as a "sprint" race. A race is classified as a "marathon" if it's 26.2 miles long, and there are rapids of varying difficulties. An "ultramarathon" is longer. A typical race is 3 to 5 miles and lasts 20 to 40 minutes. If the river is wide enough at the start, the rafts start in line; but there are very few rivers where it's possible for fifty to sixty rafts to start in this way. Timed departures are preferred, with rafts leaving every one or two minutes. Starting in line is more spectacular, but timed departures make race organization easier. In order not to be disqualified, every raft must cross the finishing line right side up, and with at least one of the crew on board.

A COLLECTIVE EXPERIENCE
During the preparations for a race and during the actual competition, the crew members share an intense collective experience. Not only must they face a series of practical operations, such as perfecting those movements that can improve their performance, but they also find themselves sharing the same fear of the river and experiencing the same feelings as others do in other athletic competitions. Rafting is, in every respect, a team sport in which emotions, satisfactions, and even possible daily disasters are shared by one and all.

RUNS
Races that take place on rivers must be lively and spectacular, but not present any objective dangers. While the starting and finishing points are always fixed, it is up to the individual crew to choose the best route.

OVERTAKING
During the run, blocking the path of another raft is not allowed. If a crew is going to be overtaken, they must let the other raft pass, or they will be disqualified.

SEATING IN A RAFT

The main difference between raft racing and recreational rafting is the paddling style. To get more leverage when racing, a position that could put the participants in difficulty for balance on board is sometimes chosen.

TEAMWORK

A crew that wants to take part in a competition must have a good mutual understanding. When the race starts improvisation is not possible and the pilots, who in the days before the race have tried the course many times over, must know exactly the best route to maneuver.

CATARAFT

These are able to offer a better performance in river races, because of their higher speed and the position of the crew on board. Also, because there is no floor they do not get weighed down by water taken on board. On the other hand, though, it is difficult to maneuver and, to make the most of its greater maneuverability, there must be perfect synchronization among the members of the crew.

Slalom

In a river slalom race, gates are hung above the river suspended from wires between the two banks, and placed so that the inflatables must follow a course that recreates characteristics of a river run. It is an artificial course that, mixed with the natural characteristics of the river, presents a challenge to the racer. In addition to the overall time for completing the course, there are time penalties for missing out or touching any of the gates.

TEAMWORK
A team running a slalom race must have a high level of mutual understanding, clear communication, and be used to maneuvering quickly and precisely, because many different types of difficulty are proposed in these races, simulating conditions found on extreme runs. Races never take place where real risks already exist for the participants.

GATES
The gates can be moved laterally or vertically from the banks in order to alter the course if there is big water. Preparation of a slalom course is a laborious and complex job.

Rafting outfitters

There are many organizations that offer tourist river runs in many parts of the world, organizing the whole trip for groups. But usually rafting outfitters are linked to a particular river where they have their base and supply inflatables, along with equipment and personnel, to lead groups down rapids. They also help and give assistance to single runners who would have difficulties with transport and recovery of an inflatable.

EVERYTHING INCLUDED
All equipment and clothing needed for the run is provided by the outfitter.

TRAINING
Every group undergoes a brief training session. It's an opportunity to start to develop a mutual understanding within the group and to realize what lays ahead on the run.

THE RUN IN GROUPS
Inflatables generally go down together in order to give any help if necessary.

RETURN TO BASE CAMP
At the end of the run there is a vehicle to take the group back to the put-in.

Outfitters based outside Europe that operate on the widest rivers are organized in a very different way from those in Europe. For a run of this type, they need to provide food and accommodation during the run. There must always be a local guide who has a complete knowledge of the river, and one or more cooks.

FACILITIES
The best outfitters are recognized by the efficiency of the guide, the pick-up after the run, and whether showers and other facilities are available.

LUXURY TREATMENT
The service provided by this type of outfitter is sometimes very luxurious. The guides set up the camps, the food is of very good quality, and the facilities offered are similar to those offered by trekking companies. In Nepal, the numerous outfitters are so competitive that they offer breaks for tea, cooked breakfasts, cakes cooked on open fires, and other little extras that tourists appreciate.

The guide

Every inflatable has a guide sitting at the back, where he has an excellent view of the river and at the same time can keep an eye on the crew. If the crew makes a mistake or cannot paddle because of the constant jolts of the raft, the guide is almost always able to control the raft on his own. The relationship that a guide establishes with the crew members is fundamental for the run. He is with people he doesn't know and only has a short time to give them the basic theory of running rapids; and he must try to guess what each individual's behavior will be in the rapids. The guide knows what to expect when running the rapids and can therefore tell the crew when they must give more, as well as give instructions – taking into account how long they might take to be carried out by the crew. For example, if, at a particular bend, the guide knows that the current will push the raft against a bank, he can tell the crew to paddle hard toward the inside of the bend well in advance. In other cases when there are particularly violent holes, rollers, and breakers, he could suggest that some, or all, of the runners hold on to the handles and stop paddling. In some situations, the guide might disguise the approaching difficulties so as not to alarm crews who are a little tense.

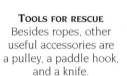

TOOLS FOR RESCUE
Besides ropes, other useful accessories are a pulley, a paddle hook, and a knife.

INSTRUCTIONS
During the run the guide must give clear instructions loud enough to be heard over the roar of the rapids and by everybody on the raft. The main instructions to the crew are: forward, back, right, left, and stop.

RESCUE ON BOARD
Sometimes a river runner can be thrown overboard, so it is up to the guide to get the person back on, and if there is an accident, to have first aid knowledge and experience in rescues.

River runners

Rafting is a group sport. Whoever takes part in a run automatically becomes part of a crew with whom the runner shares fatigue, emotions, amusement and, eventually, risks. The first run is always very emotional and people feel, physically and mentally, the grea[t] power and energy of nature. In a rapid, at the heigh[t] of emotional involvement, it is possible to see the au[-]thentic expression of each individual's character.

A UNIQUE EXPERIENCE
Sharing such an intense experience with other people, whether it's a group of friends or people you just met for the first time, is an interesting way to meet others and to discover something new within yourself.

PRELIMINARY INSTRUCTIONS
Before getting onto a raft, the runners are given instructions by the guide on the position they must take in the raft, the way they will have to paddle, and what to do in the rapids.

THE SWIMMING TEST

Before assuming responsibility for taking the crew down the river, the guide asks everyone to jump into the water to see how they react. This is also used to check the wet suits and to get used to them.

TOURIST RIVERS

In Europe, people who contact a rafting outfitter want to run a river to experience the thrill and as a challenge, while often those who choose to go with outfitters on the rivers in Asia, Africa, and the Americas want to get to know a region from a different perspective – that of a river. Sometimes people who started river running as a Sunday hobby become so enamoured that they go on more demanding runs such as on the Colorado River, or the Rio Cola, in Peru, which take a couple of weeks.

SELF-ORGANIZED TRIPS

A group of expert rafters may decide to organize a trip for themselves down one of the great rivers; in which case they could contact an outfitter there that will hire the raft, and organize transport and recovery at the end of the run.

Rafting around the world

On the most important rivers on which runs can be made there are many outfitters that can be contacted to plan a run or for any necessary assistance. These are so numerous that the fo lowing list only includes those that are know personally.

AUSTRIA

- **KARNTNER TOURISMUS**
Velden
Tel. 43-4274-52100
Fax 43-4274-5210050

- **STEIRISCHE TOURISMUS**
Graz
Tel. 43-316-4003130
Fax 43-316-40031310

- **TIROL WERBURG**
Innsbruck
Tel. 43-512-5320
Fax 43-512-5320-150

- **SALZACH AND EASTERN AUSTRIA'S RIVERS**
Niederösterreich Tourismus
Vienna
Tel. / Fax 43-222-52110

CANADA

- **ALPINE RAFTING CO. MOUNTAIN TOURS**
Golden, British Columbia
Tel. 604-344-5016

- **CANADIAN RIVER EXPEDITIONS**
Vancover, British Columbia
Tel. 604-738-4449

- **CLEARWATER EXPEDITIONS**
Kamloops, British Columbia
Tel. 604-674-3354 / 604-579-8360

- **NEW WORLD RIVER EXPEDITIONS**
Calumet, Québec
Tel. 9-242-7235/800-361-5093

CHILE

- **ALSUR**
Tel. 56-65-232334
Fax 232300

- **AQUA MOTION**
Tel./Fax 56-65-232747

- **SPORTSTOUR**
Tel. 56-2-6963100
Fax 6982981

- **TONYTOURS**
Tel./Fax 56-2-58998 / 53392

COSTA RICA

- **COSTARICA TOP TOURS**
San José
Tel. 506-296-3896-5901
Fax 506-231-7089

FRANCE

- **ISÈRE VALLEY**
Dauphiné
Tourist Office
Bourg St. Maurice
Tel. 33-4-79070492

- **DURANCE VALLEY**
Provence
Tourist Office Embrun
Tel. 33-4-924301080
Tourist Office Sisteron
Tel. 33-4-92611203

- **UBAVE VALLEY**
Provence
Tourist Office Barcelonnette
Tel. 33-4-92810368

ICELAND

- **THE BOAT PEOPLE**
Reykjavik
Tel. 354-5882900
Fax 354-5882929

ITALY

- **SCUOLA DI RAFTING DI COURMAYEUR**
Tel. 39-165-800088
Fax 39-165-809977

- **SCUOLA DI CANOA DELLA VAL SESIA**
Tel. 39-163-560957
Fax. 39-163-53552

- **AVVENTURA E NATURA**
Tel. 39-463-902990
Fax 39-463-902995

MOROCCO

- **CENTRE NATIONAL SPORTS IBNOU SINA**
Rabat
Tel./Fax 212-7-770281

MEXICO

- **PAPERO RAFTING**
Puebla
Tel./Fax 52-22-406455

NEPAL

- **DEPARTMENT OF TOURISM**
Tel. 977-1-247037-39-41-256229
Fax 977-1-1227281

NORWAY

- **NORWEGIAN WILDLIFE & RAFTING A/S**
Tel. 47-61-238727
Fax 47-61-238760

- **OPPLEY OPPDAL**
Tel. 47-74-21382
Fax 47-74-22505

PERU

- **ARTHUR TOURS**
Tel. 51-44-724489/721557

- **COLCA RAFTING REST**
Tel. 51-54-210231

- **MAJES RIVER LODGE**
Tel. 51-54-210256
For descents on the Urubanba and the Apurimac Rivers, contact any of the agencies on Plaza de Armas in Cuzco.

SLOVENIA

- **NOVEX SPORT**
Tel. 386-6532221
Fax 386-6532039

- **SOCA IRALIA**
Tel. 0481-522752
Fax 0481-522755

SPAIN

- **NOGUERA VALLEY**
Lerida
Tourist Office Sort
Tel. 34-7-3620010

SWITZERLAND

- **EUROTREK**
Tel. 41-81-4620203
Fax 41-81-4629392

- **SWISSRAFT**
Tel. 41-81-9115250
Fax 41-81-9113090

- **RHINE**
Tourist Office Scuol
Tel. 41-81-8649494
Fax 41-81-8649939

TASMANIA

- **PEREGRINE ADVENTURES**
8 Criterion Street, Hobart
Tel. 61-02-310977 Fax 348219

- **RAFTING TASMANIA**
63 Channel Highway, Taroona
Tel. 61-02-279516 Fax 279679

ZIMBABWE

- **SHEARWATER HARARE ZIMBABWE**
Tel. 263-4-735712 fax 735716

- **SHEARWATER VICTORIA FALLS**
Tel. 263-13-4471-2 fax 4341

The position on board and the paddling stroke

The paddling action is asymmetrical. Some rafters paddle on the right and others on the left, and change when they become tired. A fully-laden inflatable is quite heavy to maneuver, so the stroke needs to be decisive and deep. If, on the other hand, it is superficial and too fast, the only result is to move water and not the raft. In order to get good leverage, the sitting position must be stable and allow the upper body to lean outside the inflatable so the whole weight of the body can be put into the paddling stroke. Every paddler leans forward as much as possible from the shoulder and keeps the arm straight so that the paddle can strike the water in a decisive way. If someone finds themselves in difficulty and thinks they will be thrown out, then they should hold on to one of the handles and put the paddle in the safety position on the air chamber, taking care not to swing it about and hit one of the crew.

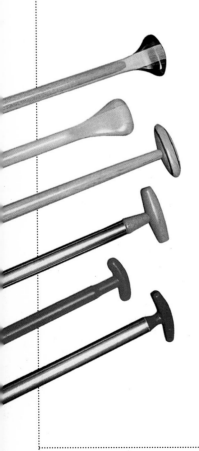

THE PADDLE
The paddle is made up of a blade, a shaft, and a T-grip. It can be made of wood or can be a composite, with an aluminium shaft and a plastic blade. The paddle is held with one hand, a hand's width from the blade, while the other holds the T-grip. The longer the shaft the greater the power of the stroke is, and therefore there is greater resistance and a more efficient paddling action. For best results, each rafter should have a paddle proportional to his height.

Canoe paddling sequence

ENTRY

POWER STROKE

EXIT

RECOVERY

POSITION ON BOARD

Half of the crew sits on the left air chamber and the other half on the right one; the guide sits at the back but to one side, paddling like the others, and at the same time steering. The rafters should not be too close together, and their legs should be inside the craft with at least one foot in the foot-straps. In races, crews are often seen sitting astride the air chamber in order to have the upper body facing downstream, and to be able to paddle with more power, but it's a very unstable and dangerous position.

IN WHITEWATER

The paddling stroke is almost the same as in quieter water, except that in the middle of the waves you have to look for the ideal place to plant the paddle and take into account the possibility of coming across a stone on its path.

Teamwork and instructions

As in canoeing, and on the old triremes, maximum efficiency is achieved when the crew plants the blade in the water in perfect unison. This timing is achieved when there is mutual understanding between the crew members. If needed, a head paddler could be nominated who keeps a constant rhythm to be followe by the crew. When there is this togetherness, th effort immediately decreases and at the same tim the raft feels lighter not only when the raft is goin forward but when reversing and during pivots.

SYNCHRONIZATION
Teamwork is very important. If all crew members are performing the same movement at the same time, they can lengthen the stroke and do the drive and exit in a more harmonious way.

OBSTACLES
When obstacles have to be passed at speed, the paddlers must try not to lose rhythm and to carry on paddling, so that the guide can foresee collisions and steer with less effort.

Maneuvers

Maneuvers that are carried out depend on the collective action of the crew in following the guide's instructions.

The guide also acts as helmsman, and his maneuvers, as a result of his position on the raft at the back, are particularly efficient. Although route for running a rapid and getting around obstacle are more or less infinite on every river, even the mos difficult can be run with the knowledge of a few ba sic maneuvers.

THE PUT-IN

If the put-in is from a quiet spot then there are no problems with starting, but if it's done in a current then a spot must be chosen where the water does not flow too fast, and the inflatable must be put in with the bow pointing upstream. While one crew member holds the raft at the bow the others get on board, check the straps and the handles, and take up the paddles. When the crew gets on board and the weight increases, the action of the river current gets more violent and it gets more difficult to hold the raft from the bank. As soon as everyone is on board, the last rafter gets on and quickly takes position.

STOPPING IN THE CURRENT

Contrary to what might be expected, if you want to stop the raft in a fast-flowing river where there are no eddies, you must not try to slow the raft by going against the flow, but head toward a spot on the bank, increasing speed as much as possible.

If the guide allows a stop, the best thing is to head downstream; it's not difficult

to see a spot where the current isn't too strong to moor. Most often the best places to stop are on the inside of a bend, rather than the outside, where the current is faster.

If it's not possible to find anywhere suitable, someone should sit on the bow and as soon as possible jump onto the bank and stop the inflatable using the mooring rope.

THE DRAW STROKE
Sometimes it may be
necessary for one of the crew
members at the front of the
raft to lean out to try and
reach a stable stretch of
water to perform a stroke
to straighten up the raft.

THE REVERSE POWER STROKE
This is performed by pushing
the back of the paddle
on the surface of the water.
It begins with the rotation
of the torso; hands remain
low; the paddle shaft is
almost parallel to the

inflatable; and the blade
is in the water in a backward
position, pushing outward
and near the water surface.
If the blade goes too
deep into the water
the recovery can be
difficult.

PIVOTING
This is used for a quick
change of direction.
As every vessel, from

a water mattress to a cruise
ship, turns more easily
at slower speeds, the guide
prepares for this turn

by slowing down and
asking the other members
to stop paddling.
To get a sudden turn to

the right, the paddlers
on the right do a reverse and
the others a forward stroke.

Rowing techniques

Better control of the raft can be obtained by using oars – especially if the boat is very heavy, as is frequently the case – when going down a river on a long expedition. This technique was initially used by the larger American outfitters, and some French ones, but has not been so popular in the rest of Europe. It consists of oars fixed to oar locks which are mounted on a special frame. Although the use of oars means that there is greater control of the inflatable when running a rapid, it could also mean that it's more dangerous for passengers when the inflatable is jolted by waves.

THE FRAME
The frame, which is usually made of metal and is fixed to the inflatable by means of straps and rings, acts as a support for the oars and stiffens the raft so that a seat and a foot brace can be added and is also used for loading and stowing baggage.

A WOODEN FRAME
Hand-made frames can be mounted on inflatables and on catarafts made by the rafter.

REAR FRAMES
The frame can be mounted at the stern so that the guide can check the load and the passengers and act promptly in an emergency.

OARS

Oars used for rafting are either made of wood or plastic and aluminium and are about 10 feet (3 m) long. Their length means that with the minimum of effort the leverage of the stroke is more powerful, especially in a pivot.

DANGERS

In narrow rivers with a lot of whitewater, the oars could hit rocks, which is potentially dangerous.

OAR LOCKS

Mounted on the inflatable, they are made in such a way that they release if they hit rocks on the riverbed.

In rapids

The difference between running rapids rationally and running them by chance is having complete control of the direction and a strategy. There are some dangerous situations that it's better to avoid, such as entrapments in places impossible to reach from land and where it's difficult to carry out a rescue. There are certain types of rapids where it's known that the inflatable will be pushed to places on the river best avoided, like the outside of a bend, dangerous narrow parts, and places where tree roots stick out into the river. When the guide has a good idea of the route to take, then it isn't difficult to carry out maneuvers to maintain it. The most basic thing to do is to keep the raft on the main line of the current and anticipate any corrections to avoid collisions with obstacles. On larger rivers, many different possibilities may exist, and it's not always easy to decide on the best route to take to avoid any problems.

WAVES
In confluences and at the start of a current there is a moment in which the raft could be broadside to the current and a wave could swamp or even flip it over. In cases like this, every member of the crew should shift their weight downstream; it is difficult for the current to knock over the inflatable upstream.

ENTRAPMENT/WRAP
If the inflatable gets stuck on rocks leaving the main current, almost always, the crew has to get out and push downstream. Sometimes, removing the weight of two people is enough to lighten the raft sufficiently. As soon as it starts to move again, it's necessary to be ready to jump back on board.

CUTTING THE BEND

Centrifugal forces naturally push the inflatable to the outside of a bend and it's very difficult to get back to the main current. To neutralize this effect it's a good idea to anticipate by pushing the raft to the inside of every bend.

HOLES

Sometimes a raft can get caught in a hole that is difficult to get out of. In a case like this, the weight needs to be directed downstream, and try to reach the deep current with the blades.

AVOIDING HOLES

If the raft is facing the wrong direction and there is no time to straighten before a hole or roller, rather than finishing broadside, it's better to meet it straight on. At the first possible moment, the raft position can be corrected by rotating the bow downstream.

STEERING FROM THE REAR

Typical movements carried out only by the guide are steering from the rear and straightening the stern. Both of these are used to change the trajectory suddenly. They are so efficient that the guide can direct the raft independently of what the other crew members are doing.

Transport and recovery of the raft

One of the main organizational obstacles to the practice of a sport is transport of the equipment used and the recovery of the crew and their gear after the run. For skiing there are ski lifts, but for rafting, vehicles must be used which take the runners and the inflatables back to the put-in. Runs organized by outfitters provide this service, but for self-organized runs friends or relatives must help out and agree to a meeting point accessible by road, or, in the worst scenario, use trains or buses, or even hitch-hike. Unlike a rigid canoe, an inflatable can be quickly deflated and folded up.

LARGE OUTFITTERS
These operate on the bigger rivers all over the world, such as Shotover in New Zealand, which organizes transport and recovery of tens of rafts at a time.

SMALLER OUTFITTERS
European and other outfitters tend to be smaller and use minibuses but have a more friendly atmosphere.

TRUCKS
In Siberia, where rafters have to travel hundreds of miles to get to a river, they use any means at their disposal to solve the problem of transporting inflatables.

PORTAGING
Sometimes it's necessary to portage the raft because of various obstacles and impossible river conditions, such as dams, waterfalls, siphons, or dangerous rapids. In these cases the weight should be well distributed depending on the height of the people.

HELICOPTERS
Ex-military helicopters are an ingenious system used in Siberia to reach rivers inaccessible by land.

MOTORIZED DELTAPLANE
On the Flumendosa River in Sardinia, Italy, someone has even devised a way of reaching an inaccessible river by using a motorized deltaplane to transport a canoe.

FERRYING MEANS
The inflatable can also be used for transporting heavy loads without damaging the structure.

Hand and paddle signals

All river runners must know some basic signals, which were elaborated in the United States, to communicate from a distance. Frequently the roar of the rapid makes it impossible to hear any verbal communication. Please note that these signals are subject to change from one river to another.

PERSON OVERBOARD
Raising and lowering the paddle vertically indicates that someone has fallen into the water. At the same time indicate the position in the water.

RAFT DAMAGED
Forming a circle with the hands raised above your head signals a damaged raft.

WRAP
Putting both hands on the forehead indicates that the raft is entrapped.

HURRY UP
When it is important to hurry up move your forearm in a circular movement.

EVERYTHING IS OKAY
When there is nothing to stop the raft run, raise your hand over your head.

FIRST AID
When help and a first aid kit are needed, make a cross with your forearms.

PORTAGING
If it's necessary to portage the raft along the bank, raise your hand over your shoulder, with the palm facing upward.

STOP
In case of danger, make a sign with your hand up and facing outward to stop an approaching raft. Alternately, hold the paddle horizontally over your head or hold your arms out straight to sides.

Dangers on the river

The biggest danger is being thrown overboard and finding yourself in the whitewater at the mercy of the current. For this reason, every rafter, besides knowing how to swim and being correctly equipped, must know what to do in these circumstances. The most important thing is not to panic when being pulled under water by rollers, whirlpools and waves.

SWIMMING IN A RIVER
If you fall in the water, you should take up the safety position, lying on your back with feet held high and pointed downstream. Try to keep hold of the paddle, as you may not be able to get it back later. Never try to stand up or walk, even if the water is shallow, because it is impossible to go against the current and a foot could get stuck in between the rocks on the riverbed.

RECOVERY ON BOARD
In this type of emergency, the guide must give instructions to get close to the swimmer, preferably downstream, hopefully avoiding him and being careful not to crush him between a rock and the raft. The rafter in the best position on the raft should help the swimmer to get back on board, sticking out the paddle to help.

THE RAFT LEANS OVER

When the raft leans over rafters who are not holding on tightly could be thrown out. These situations can be avoided by looking ahead at the river course.

HOLES

If the raft is stopped by a hole downstream of a rock then all the weight of the crew must be shifted downstream and at the same time try to get back to the main current by planting the blade vertically and deeply. To get closer to the current you can move the bow or stern of the inflatable.

THE RAFT FLIPS OVER

When the raft flips over somebody could remain underneath. There is no need to panic, because there is enough room to breathe under the inflatable, and, by pushing yourself away energetically, it's not difficult to free yourself.

Rescue during a race

If someone falls overboard during a race, they may be lucky enough to be picked up by one of the rescue teams, which are usually placed in the more difficult stretches of the river.

Throwing the rope

The use of a rope for a rescue is limited to land-based rescues; it's useless to throw a rope from an inflatable when you can go to the person to be rescued. A rope tied to a raft risks getting snagged on something and can be dangerous. The rescuer uses a throw bag, in which the rope is stowed and which is designed to spool out freely when it's tossed.

THE RESCUE
Two people are usually enough to carry out a rescue on a river that is not too wide. One of them, with a harness attached to the rope, goes into the river, while the other person on the bank holds the other end of the rope.

THE RECOVERY
With great care, the person on the bank pulls his companion toward the bank, taking care to do so without jerking the rope and looking for a good place where they can climb up.

MAN ON A LEAD
This is where the rescuer must jump in as soon as he sees his companion re-emerge and is sure of being able to catch hold of him by the torso.

The throwing sequence

THE POSITION
Before throwing, it's important to find a place with good footing on the rock and, if possible, dry. There must be a grab loop at the end of the rope to hold tightly.

METHOD
Prepare for the throw by fixing on the point where you want to throw the rescue bag. For an efficient throw, try to avoid hitting branches and bushes and other obstacles.

A LONG THROW
Especially during a rescue in a rapid, a long throw that isn't so accurate is better than a throw that is not far enough to reach the person in the water.

THE ROPE
If the rope has been inserted properly it will spool out freely. For a more accurate throw, it's a good idea to fix a carabiner to the end to make it heavier.

THE SECOND THROW
It is possible to toss the rope again without reinserting it in the bag, which can be thrown with the water-filled bag.

Rollers

When there's a steep change in the gradient of the riverbed, rollers are formed, which are breaking waves with a lot of foam, a circular surface movement, and which fall back upstream on themselves. If the mass of water is big, it can be powerful enough to keep any floating object trapped; sometimes it can even flip over an inflatable and its crew. If you arrive at a high speed and paddle decisively, it's possible to go through the breaker and get past the obstacle. If, on the other hand, you are broadside to the current, it's more difficult to carry on.

When the bow hits the roller, the crew is often covered by waves and in this case it is advisable to hold on to the handles. If the raft is flipped over, the roller is more likely to keep the inflatable than the crew. Because the raft floats on the surface, it's more susceptible to the effect of the roller, whereas the crew members falling toward the riverbed are pushed downstream by the faster flow of the current. On some rivers with big water it's possible to see flipped-over rafts that are trapped by a roller. Usually when this happens the crew is able to reach the bank a little farther downstream, but have problems in recovering the raft. To reach it a pole with a hook is not always enough because of the width of the river. The one consolation is that sooner or later the roller will send the raft downstream.

Wraps or entrapments

This is when a raft is pinned against an obstacle by river currents. The power of even a quiet river should not be underestimated. It is always possible to cause a wrap that is difficult to get out of because the mass of water is acting on the whole side of the raft. A wrap is the riskiest situation that can happen when running a rapid because a crew member could become trapped between the rock and the inflatable. This is why any non-necessary rigging, accessory, or baggage should not be stowed. If a wrap happens, the crew should free themselves from the straps and get onto the obstacle before the inflatable is submerged by the current. After having given the necessary instructions, the guide should start measures to get out of this situation.

A wrap against rocks

The crew is almost always able to get onto the rocks that have caused the wrap. Sometimes the guide, with the help of some crew members, is able to push one end of the raft upstream; other times he will decide it is necessary to use ropes from the bank. The important thing is to cause a deformation or change its position in order to free it. An expert guide can even use the push of the water pillow upstream of the rock. In any case, it's easier to free a self-bailing inflatable than one with a conventional tub floor that fills up with water.

A wrap against tree trunks

It can be even more difficult than against rocks because the floating trunks do not obstruct the flow, but make it flow faster under them. The crew is exposed to more dangers because it's more difficult to find a safe place. It's impossible to free a raft full of baggage and people; so you should try to fix a static rope to help reach the bank.

Flipping over

An inflatable can only flip over if there is a certain current, and this is a rare occurrence. It usually happens where there is a big roller, a violent crash against something, or when there are diagonal waves and all the crew is on the same side of the raft.

Sometimes in very choppy rapids some members of the crew can be thrown out of position and cause all the people on that side of the raft to land heavily on the tube.

To avoid flipping over they should get back into position as quickly as possible. To increase safety, it's better for groups of inflatables to run the rapids so that if there is a possibility of flipping over, the other rafts waiting below can offer assistance.

Flipping over sequence 1

Flipping over sequence 2

River rescue

The fire department and professional river rescue organizations intervene with modern safety techniques if there is an accident or there are floods. Inflatables, wetsuits, and rafting helmets allow them, in an emergency, to come to the rescue of people and rafts.

RECOVERY ON THE BANK
When it is not possible to upright the raft it's better to get on top and paddle to the shore.

UPRIGHTING
Whoever recovers an inflatable, whether a guide or a fireman, must have about 10 feet of rope, with a carabiner at one end to be able to upright the inflatable after climbing on top. It is very important to remember to keep hold of the paddle without it there would be no sense getting back on board

The uprighting sequence

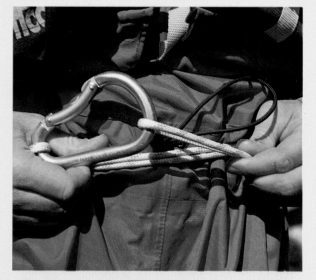

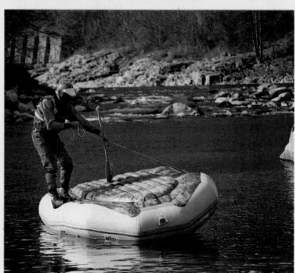

The use of ropes

In a rescue situation it's very useful to know how to use a rope. Somebody who is not used to using one will have difficulty if it gets entangled. During a rescue you can't afford to lose time fumbling with a tangled rope.

COILING

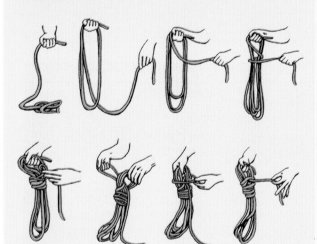

The best way to coil a rope was developed by sailors and climbers: we can learn some useful tricks from them for a rescue.

QUICK COILING

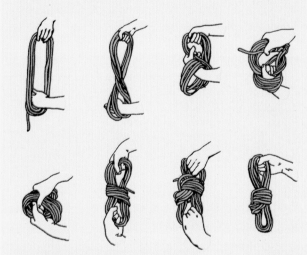

This method is quicker than the previous way: experts can tie knots and do recoiling with only one hand as well as in difficult situations.

HOIST AND PULLEYS

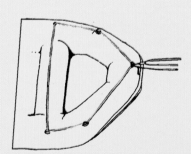

The hoist used to free a raft needs a good support place on land. It's better to use a static rope and pulleys that are not too small. This particular system is mechanically very efficient .

Running the Sun Kosi River

It started with a wish to get away from it all. Some friends got together and a discussion started about where to go. The Colorado River is the first one that comes to mind, but you have to book the run a long time in advance. The Rio Colca is beautiful but there are some extreme rapids, and the Zambezi is too frequented by tourists. In the end just one name satisfied everyone: the Sun Kosi, which in Nepalese means "Golden River." The run lasts nine days and goes through a very interesting region in terms of its nature and people. There are no roads along the Sun Kosi, and the river is the only access to places still impossible to explore other than on foot or by mule.

THE KAYAKS
The transport of the kayaks, which along with the rafts and hydrospeed were needed for the run down the Sun Kosi, was a little more complicated: we had to rent rickshaws.

KATHMANDU
In Nepal there are about fifty companies organizing rafting, not only on the Sun Kosi, but also on the Trisuli, the Marsjandi, the Karnali, and on other rivers. The agency that we'd booked in advance rented a minibus on which the rafts, provisions, and baggage were loaded.

BUYING PROVISIONS
A must were the markets in Kathmandu. As a result of having to travel for nine days, it was necessary to buy most of the provisions.

In some of the villages on the river run, it was possible to find potatoes, mandarins, biscuits, sometimes beer, soya seeds to chew, but little else.

THE SUN KOSI SPRINGS
These are found in Tibet, but after a few miles the river is in Nepalese territory, where a bridge marks one of the most important frontiers between the two countries.

THE PUT-IN
Before sunset there were several hours of a manageable road, though it was not without some difficulties that we reached the put-in on the banks of the Sun Kosi where the first camp was set up. The real adventure of the run started the next morning.

THE TEMPLE ON THE RIVER
Most Nepalese are Hindus, but there are many Buddhists nearer to the Himalayan slopes, where there are a lot of temples with Tibetan prayer wheels.

BRIDGES
The last road on the Sun Kosi is the bridge that marks the point beyond which all signs of modern life are left behind. For 87 miles (140 km) you only come across small villages and suspended bridges.

On the river

PERMITS
The following morning the expedition is ready to leave but is held up by a police check. In Nepal, for security reasons, you cannot run a river without special permits – which are issued in Kathmandu – and a local guide.

THE FIRST RAPID
The Sun Kosi meanders quietly. On the banks there are groups of monkeys, which seem to be acting as spies on this strange procession of rafts, canoes, and hydrospeeds. Then, suddenly, we can hear the telltale roar of the first rapid. The waves are over 7 feet (2 m) high and the rollers are very powerful, but the rafts keep the ideal route nonetheless.

THE GUID
Chitra knows the rive like the back of hi hand and knows th best places to pitc the tents at sunset With him there is cook. Frequently th guide and cook ar sherpas who have th same job for trekkin and climbing in th Himalayas. They ar more used to workin on land and som of them canno swim

THE RUN
Very soon the members of the expedition realize that they are dealing with a river with different characteristics from those they are normally used to – both because of the length of the rapids and the wild countryside they are going through.

THE FERRYMEN
As we proceed we go through more sparsely populated regions than the rest of Nepal.

Where there is a village or the river intersects a path there are ferrymen with their typical canoes.

THE DUDH KOSI
VALLEY
One of the main tributaries of the "Golden River" is the Dudh Kosi. We come across the confluence of this river from the north on the sixth day.

MOUNT EVEREST
The glaciers of Everest feed the Dudh Kosi which is freezing cold and turbulent. This river has one of the longest and most difficult whitewater rapids in the world, stretching for 62 miles (100 km) and which cannot be run in an inflatable, but they have been run by some in canoes.

THE WATER LEVEL OF THE RIVER
During the rainy season it increases by as much as 33 feet (10 m). To avoid any problems, the best time to run the river is at the end of the monsoon, which lasts until September. The best months are October, November, and December. In January it is possible to do rafting, but the days are very short and there is the risk of spending a lot of time in the tent.

SUSPENDED BRIDGES
They are characteristic of the Nepalese countryside. In nearly all the valleys, the old bridges made from hemp and bamboo have been replaced by more solid constructions using steel cables.

USING OTHER MEANS
The hydrospeeds and the kayaks can be very amusing but also very demanding in the rapids that the rafts run without any problems. During this run, the members of the crew tried out different means.

The campsite

THE CHOICE OF THE SITE

Every day we ran about 9 miles (15 km) and spent about three to four hours on the inflatable. The fog on the river didn't lift much before ten o'clock and in early afternoon we had to start looking for a campsite for the night. The guide knew many of the best places for the sun, sandy beaches, and where to find wood easily for the fire.

UNLOADING THE BAGS

Every evening there was the same routine of drying the wet suits and unloading the bags; the next morning it was necessary to stow everything on board in dry bags.

DINNER

As soon as wood was found and the fire lit, Dundee, the cook, prepared dinner. Sitting around the fire eating became one of the rituals that characterized everyday life.

VISITS

When pitching the tents, very frequently young children and adults would seem to appear from nowhere, curious about the strangers.

VENDORS

Along the paths of Nepal there are many people who are traveling on foot taking their merchandise from one part of the country to the other. Usually they come from the north and are taking produce grown in the mountains down into the valleys; after selling it they buy hand-made goods and other goods which they take home or sell on their way. It was an opportunity for us to buy fruit, other food products and even Nepalese objects.

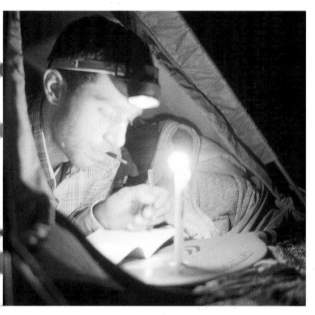

IN THE OPEN
Those who do not want to sleep in the tent can sleep in the open, as the Nepalese guides usually do.

At night the humidity is very high, but the inflatable propped up by two oars it offers excellent protection.

IN THE TENT
When night falls, those who want to read must make do with a candle, a flashlight, or a kerosene lamp.

MORNING
At dawn the humidity has created an opal-colored fog which only lifts when the sun has risen high. You have to force yourself to get out of the tent, but washing in the river soon wakes you up. The cooks prepare breakfast, and fortified, we break camp.

GOOD-BYES
After the rafters have loaded the inflatables it's not uncommon for the people whom we'd met the evening before to come and say goodbye, and distract themselves from their chores started at dawn. One of the traditional chores for young girls is to fetch water every morning from the springs.

Arrival

THE SUN KOSI GORGE

We crossed it in the last part of the journey. They are famous for the series of violent rapids caused by the great mass of water going through two great walls of rock. Before running them, it's a good idea to scout them to get a better idea of their conformation.

THE JOURNEY COMES TO AN END

After having gone through the most feared difficulty, the rafters begin to realize that the run is coming to an end. The sense of time had been profoundly changed: it had been following that of the river and the count of the days had been lost, but soon the routine life will start again.

CHATTRA

The signs of civilization become more evident: street lights and an excavator on the riverbed appear almost surreal. The outfitter's vehicles are waiting to pick up the inflatables and the crew. The trip back to Kathmandu will take about twenty hours.

THE ARUN AND THE TAMUR

The confluence of these two rivers appeared on the last day of the run. They are both very long rivers that originate in the Himalayan glaciers and can be run in either inflatables or in kayaks. The Arun runs through one of the deepest and most interesting canyons in the world.

BARACETRA
The Temple of Baracetra indicates in a very suggestive way the end of the journey; the white stands out against the vegetation and is visible from a few miles.

Italy

By now, dams, conduits, barrages, and artificial embankments have changed the courses of all the alpine rivers and of almost all their torrents, while excavations have altered their riverbeds. Those rivers that have not dried up completely have had their flows impoverished and no longer guarantee the conservation of the environment essential for the survival of acquatic species. Man's interests have also been damaged: since rivers are no longer self-purifying and their surface waters no longer oxygenated, the fishing industry has suffered. What is more, a process of hydrogeological unbalance has been set into action, often causing disastrous floods. As one of the very few rivers that has remained relatively untouched by man, the Sesia deserves special protection – as does its famous camp-school for rafting and kayaking – with its wide and deep rapids, transparent waters, and verdant landscapes.

The Arkansas River

On this river, a couple of hours drive from Denver, there is a secluded town called Texas Creek, where a put-in for inflatables starts at 24 miles (38 km). The Arkansas River is very well-known to local river runners. Many rafting organizations in the area organize all-inclusive, one- or two-day trips. In the first part of the run the river flows fast without any great difficulties, then from the halfway point there are some Class IV and V rapids.

After this, the river enters a gorge where the difficulty remains at the same level, but the water volume becomes greater.

Africa

On the African continent there are few areas for whitewater rafting. Some examples include the rivers that flow into the Atlantic in Morocco, the various tributaries of the Nile, the Omo, and the Zambezi. In Morocco, some fast rivers like the Dades flow toward the Atlantic along arid and little-inhabited valleys, but an occasional Arab or Berber village can be seen. The Blue Nile and the White Nile are the main confluences on which rafting can be practiced.

The Omo, in Ethiopia, is not very exciting from a rafting point of view, but it's very interesting from an ethnographic one, because it goes through hundreds of miles of villages inhabited by many different peoples. The Zambezi River, in Zimbabwe, downstream from the Victoria Falls, is one of the most visited places for rafting.

Even in South Africa there are many interesting runs like the Unkomaas, which is still not very well-known by whitewater rafters.

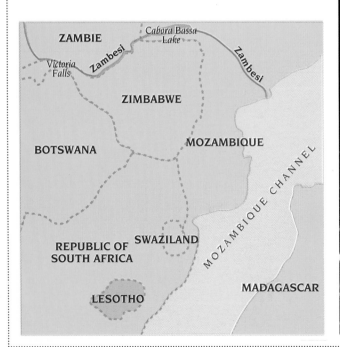

Patagonia

The ambition of many European and North American canoeists and rafters in winter is to move to the rivers in the Southern Hemisphere. In South America there are rivers of every type. The Andean rivers, such as the Urubamba, the Rio Colca, and the Apurimac, start at over 20,000 feet (6,000 m) and have very steep gradients. The rivers in the Amazon Basin, like those in Ecuador, Bolivia, and Colombia, have a big flow and run through areas of very thick vegetation, and it is not always easy to find access to a put-in.

In Patagonia, at the extreme south of the continent, the river network is very rich. Even though in this zone the gradients in the Andes are not as steep as in the north, the rapids are exceptional. There are many famous rivers such as the Bio Bio and less well-known ones like the Rio Mans.

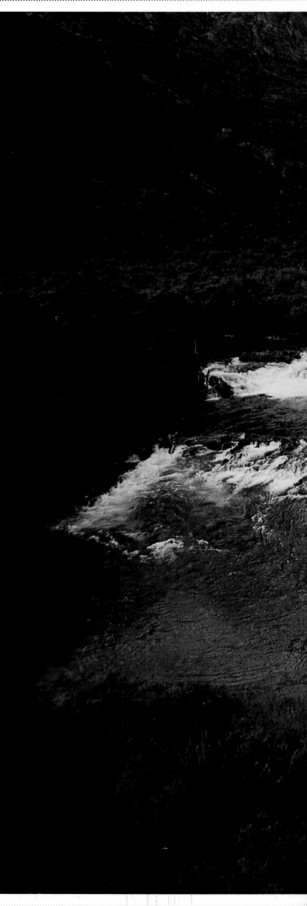

Canada

A seventh of the fresh water in the world is found in Canada, and as a result it is known as the land of lakes and rivers. The main limit to rafting in this region is the short duration of the thaw. The Canadian rafting companies do not work more than two or three months a year, and very frequently in the winter period they organize trips to Central America.

In Canada, rafting and canoeing are very popular sports, so much so that it is possible to find a canoe in almost every household. There are also many waterplanes that transport people and equipment to put-ins on rivers and lakes.

On rivers like the Yukon, the Fraser, and the Mackenzie, runs of several hundred miles are possible, repeating trips made by the Indians and the first explorers. The main areas that are crossed during a run are sparsely populated and meeting other river runners can be a pleasant experience.

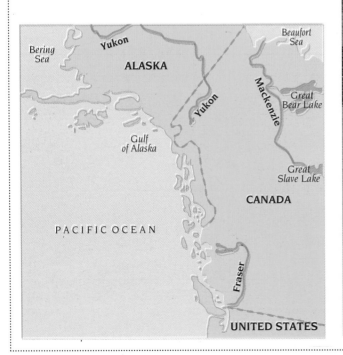

Glossary

BANK: The river's shore.

BIG WATER: Refers to rivers with large volume and powerful hydraulics.

BLADE: The wide, flat part of a paddle or oar.

BOW: The front or nose of an inflatable.

BREAKING WAVE: A standing wave that falls upstream.

CARABINER: A metal clip used to attach lines to inflatables, to secure gear, or to substitute for a pulley.

CHUTE: A narrow, constricted portion of the river.

CLASSIFICATION: A system for rating the difficulty of whitewater rapids.

CONFLUENCE: The point where two rivers or streams meet.

CURRENT: Moving water.

DROP: A steep, sudden change in the level of the river bottom.

DRY BAG: A waterproof bag designed to keep its contents dry.

DRY SUIT: A waterproof suit that encloses a paddler in impermeable layers of fabric. Designed to be worn over insulating layers of clothing.

EDDY: A pocket of water downstream of an obstacle that flows upstream or back against the current.

ENTRAPMENT: A situation in which an inflatable gets pinned against an obstacle by the river's current.

GRADIENT: A term used to measure a river's descent.

HOLE: A swirling vortex of water wherein the river pours over an obstacle and drops toward the riverbed, leaving a pocket behind the obstacle that is filled in by an upstream surface current.

LIFEJACKET: A personal flotation device designed to float a swimmer in water.

PILLOW: A cushion of water that forms on the upstream side of an obstacle.

PIVOT: To turn the inflatable in place.

PORTAGE: To carry an inflatable around a rapid.

PUT-IN: The place where an inflatable trip begins.

ROLLER: A big curling wave that falls back upstream on itself.

SCOUT: To walk along a bank to inspect the river.

SELF-BAILING: A type of inflatable that lets water drain out through the floor.

TAKE-OUT: The place where an inflatable trip ends and inflatables depart from the river.

THROW BAG: A bag that holds a long coiled rope, used as a rescue device to be tossed to swimmers.

THWART: The cross-tube of an inflatable.

WRAP: An inflatable pinned flat against an obstacle by river currents.

EDITOR: Maurizio Bernasconi

PHOTOGRAPHY EDITOR: Marco Tenucci

TRANSLATION: Richard Land

PHOTOS: Annapaola Agati, Francesco Balducci,
Emanuele Bernasconi, Maurizio Bernasconi, Elena Bruschi,
Alberto Campanile, Giorgio Caniato, Marco Capovilla, Enrico Caracciolo,
Rinaldo Del Fante, Massimiliano Dorigo, Eugenio Ferrari, Roberto Ferrero,
Riccardo Fiocchini, Martino Frova, Andrea Gatti, Edoardo Ghelma,
Guido Guri, The Image Bank, Paolo Lovatto, Marco Majrani, Eugenio Manghi,
Marco Melodia, Giorgio Mesturini, Aris Mihich,
Renato Murgolo, Vittorio Pongolini, Gianluca Ricci, Valentina Scaglia, Paolo Simoncelli,
Mario Soster, Marco Tenucci, Bruno Zanzottera

COVER: Pentagram

Thanks for the collaboration:
Associazione Acquaviva, Milano; Canoa Club, Milano;
Hidronica, Varallo Sesia (Vercelli); Rainbow Kayaks, Bergamo;
Scuola di canoa e rafting, Morgex (Aosta); Vigili del fuoco, Pavia;
W.B.I. Italia - Camel Trophy; Zodiac Italia, Milano

LAYOUT: Luca Theodoli

DRAWINGS: Simona Ferri

PRODUCTION: Ready-made, Milano

First published in the United States of America in 1998
by UNIVERSE PUBLISHING
A Division of Rizzoli International Publications, Inc.
300 Park Avenue South
New York, NY 10010

© 1998 RCS Libri S.p.A.

98 99 00 01 02/ 10 9 8 7 6 5 4 3 2 1

Printed in Italy

Library of Congress Card Catalogue Number 98-61138
ISBN O-7893-0221-7

Maurizio Bernasconi was born in Milan in 1955
and is one of the best known Italian canoeists.
After participating in the 1973 World
Championship, he went on to win a number
of competitions and, in 1978, founded the Scuola
di canoa della Valsesia (Valsesia Canoe School)
that was the first to introduce rafting in Italy.
He published *La tecnica del kayak* in 1986
and *Canoa, kayak, rafting, torrentismo* in 1995.

Marco Tenucci was born in Florence in 1956
and holds a degree in natural science.
He is both a reporter and photographer,
and is editor in chief of the Italian magazine
Itinerari e luoghi. He has taken part in several
rafting competitions, has run rivers all over
the world and is the author
of geographic and naturalistic publications.